BLURRED ENCOUNTERS

BLURRED ENCOUNTERS

A reasoned practice of faith

JOHN READER

Aureus

First published in 2005 by
Aureus Publishing Limited

ISBN 1-899750-35-5

A catalogue record for this book is available from the British Library.

Typeset by Andrew Buckley, Clunton, Shropshire.

Printed and bound in Great Britain.

Aureus Publishing Limited
Castle Court
Castle-upon-Alun
St Bride's Major
Vale of Glamorgan
CF32 0TN

Tel: 01656 880033
International Tel/Fax: (+044) 1656 880033

E-mail: sales@aureus.co.uk
Website: www.aureus.co.uk

Contents

Aureus Studies in Post-Foundational Theology

This series aims to articulate a new and developing approach to the relationship between the Christian tradition and contemporary culture. Rather than seeing this as a clash between metanarratives each built upon firm and incontrovertible foundations the various texts explore the possibilities for a relationship between traditions more guarded and humble in their claims to truth. This does not mean that the frameworks and assumptions are no longer of any value but that they need to be treated as contingent and provisional. This approach has a particular significance for practical engagement, whether pastorally, politically or socially based and is thus of value for developing a public theology at a time when Christianity's credibility outside its own boundaries is in considerable doubt.

Other books in the series:

Beyond All Reason: The limits of post-modern theology
John Reader, 1997
ISBN 1-899750-02-9

Agape, Moral Meaning and Pastoral Counselling
Simon Robinson, 2001
ISBN 1-899750-09-6

Truth and Scripture: Challenging underlying assumptions
Brenda Watson, 2004
ISBN 1-899750-27-4

All published by Aureus Publishing Limited

Acknowledgements

As is the case with any text of this nature, a wide variety of people have, knowingly or unknowingly, played a part in its creation. I would like to acknowledge a number of different groups, some academically based and others more practically orientated who have shared the journey at various points.

Some of the theoretical material is derived from my doctorate for the University of Wales, Bangor and my supervisor, John Heywood Thomas, was a constant source of encouragement and critical reflection during that process. This coincided with the brief existence of the International Research Institute for Spirituality and Change (IRISC) for which friends at Bangor and beyond provided a forum for debate, including the subjects of the Foot and Mouth outbreak and spiritual development. So my thanks to fellow IRISCERS, the Revd Ian Ball, Dr John Fazey, Simon Parker, the Revd Dr Ian Carter, the Revd Jeff Leonardi, the Revd Margaret Goodall, and Dr Caroline Baillie.

Manchester University in the person of Dr Elaine Graham, the Revd Dr Chris Baker from the William Temple Foundation and, most notably, Canon Dr John Atherton, formerly Canon Theologian at the Cathedral, also remain as central discussion partners for much of this material. John in particular has worked through the whole text and been unswerving in his support for the project. All three are now engaged in establishing the Manchester Centre for Public Theology, along with others from the North West Region, which I believe will be a significant base for further contextually-based theology.

I would also like to mention some friends and correspondents from Lancaster University who have helped on matters environmental and on tracing some philosophical sources: Dr Bron Szerszynski who commissioned the article for Ecotheology which forms the basis for Chapter 6, Dr Clare Palmer and Dr Alison Stone.

For the more practical and local involvements I pay tribute to Guy Weston, now Chief Executive of Festival Housing Group and other colleagues from the Housing Association world (Guy did read some of this!). Also colleagues and friends from the Worcestershire Industrial Mission and others whom I have encountered while working for WIM, especially Sascha McDonald of Community Action, Wyre Forest, who put me on to some of the material in Chapter 1. Then there was the group which met locally to discuss the aftermath of the Foot and Mouth outbreak and particularly Laurence McCurrich who has again shared some of the ideas in the book. Then others from the Four Square Parishes, especially those involved in the Children's Festivals and the Toddlers Group, all of the committee members from both of those projects including Rachel Wyatt, Nicki Maxted and Lisa Barrett and then particularly Jacqueline Allen who also organized the Toddlers into producing the cover for the book. Thanks also to Matthew Blackbourn (*www.blacksalmon.co.uk*) for help in adapting the picture for publication. My wife and children for interesting input along the way, Christine and Kate on the children's work, Simon on philosophy and the environment (apples especially), and Tom now pursuing globalization at Manchester.

Finally, to my friend going back further than all the rest, Andrew Buckley, for continuing conversations on all matters and, not least, for typesetting the text, a massive thanks for his support and commitment over those years.

Introduction

There is a famous wartime film called *Brief Encounter* (1945). A significant section of the action takes place at a railway station where two people, both already married, begin a relationship that is ultimately doomed to disappointment and frustration. As the write-up on the video packaging says: 'It is the story of two people, thrown together by the chance meeting of the title, helpless in the face of their emotions but redeemed by their moral courage'. Within the parameters of their contemporary morality this relationship constitutes an 'affair' even though it does not develop into the long term. The background music is taken from Rachmaninov's Second Piano Concerto. The clock on the platform of Carnforth station in Lancashire is an enduring image of this relationship marking the passing of time which must tear all connections apart. From this idea of the brief encounter I have adopted and adapted my own title to that of *Blurred Encounters* as an attempt to describe my experience of the relationship between the Christian tradition and contemporary social action. I need to explain why I have done this.

One explanation is that what I am writing about is a relationship or a set of relationships. One could argue that this might be a relationship between two theories or even two institutions but I would want to say that it is only human beings who truly encounter one another. For that reason everything is personal. I will repeat: everything is personal, even though humans construct theories and structures in which to wrap up their experiences. What I will be talking about in this book are relationships between different groups of people, between different individuals and within the individuals themselves. Within such relationships there is a range of possible connections. At one extreme there is no relationship – two people pass each other underneath the clock but no encounter takes place. At the other extreme they encounter each other in such a way that one 'partner' then dominates or takes over the other. In between there is a spectrum of blurred encounters where each may be changed but may also retain an integrity within that process. Real encounter, I am arguing, must risk compromise, appropriation, a potential loss of identity and integrity, whatever the final outcome. This describes my experience of trying to engage with practical issues from within the Christian tradition.

Is this theology? For those who might be troubled by such a question I would argue that it is and I would hope that this book will support that argument. On one level I write this as a personal story. It could have been a novel but I do not have the skills to produce that. From the midst of the personal stories emerge certain key themes or questions which then lead me to draw upon a range of resources as I attempt to interpret, understand and justify the activities in which I have engaged. I am aware that there are weighty theoretical arguments about different ways of 'doing theology', but I do not want to refer to these in any detail here. I will however try to locate my approach for the benefit of others. 'Contextual' is a term that I might have used a few years ago. When I wrote *Local Theology* (Reader 1994) in the early 1990s I believed that I was trying to produce a contextual theology from an essentially rural setting to show that such an approach did not necessarily have to based in an urban context. The next book, *Beyond All Reason* (Reader 1997), contained a more substantial engagement with some theoretical resources that I then labeled 'postmodern' but was still an attempt to struggle with the question of how to relate the Christian tradition to contemporary ideas and issues. This time around I have deliberately written a text that straddles and blurs the boundary between practice and theory in a number of ways. It is a blurred encounter between the practical and the theoretical and this is the way in which I believe things have to develop.

I have also 'toyed' in recent years with the term 'Post-Foundational' as a way of trying to do justice to this way of working. Hence I would want to place my work broadly within a process that Brenda Watson (Aureus 2004) has described in the previous book in this series. She is concerned to argue that the search for truth needs to acknowledge the provisionality and contingency of all our conclusions.

> Partial and provisional certainty is the only realistic goal, for knowledge can never get beyond challengeability except in the most trivial or ordinary matters. The search for truth can utilize all ways of knowing without capitulating to obsessive reductionism.
> (Watson 2004, 180)

In my words, we just have to be cautious and guarded about our claims to truth, particularly when it comes to talking about human identity and indeed about God. That seems to me a sound theological position which recognizes the limitations of what we can come to understand about the meaning of human life.

However, I would not want people to get 'hung-up' on either of these terms, contextual or Post-Foundational. Such words are all too rapidly appropriated or absorbed by the industry of academic theology and then become remote from the practice in which some of us are engaged. I would prefer that there were no labels, but I accept that these are sometimes useful ways of helping others to locate and identify what it is that they encounter.

Finally I should position this book in relationship to the tradition of social or public theology that I associate particularly with Manchester Cathedral, diocese and University, including especially John Atherton and successive friends from the William Temple Foundation. I hope that this text will contribute to the developing discussions on the theme of social capital and the possible role for faith traditions in the tasks of neighbourhood and community renewal and voluntary welfare provision. The government has now set up a Faith Communities Unit as a Home Office initiative and begun to produce the usual tranche of documents and reports to which religious groupings are expected to respond (*Church Times*, 2 April 2004). How this encounter develops will be of significance over the coming months. Most responses will probably emerge from the urban or inner city context. That is not where I am located. Again I hesitate to label and define since it will probably create misconceptions, but one could call my context now 'ex-urban'; on the fringes of a conurbation yet neither strictly urban nor traditionally rural. Another argument I want to defend is that there are no privileged locations for 'doing theology', just different ones from which similar but also distinct themes and questions will probably emerge.

So this is the story of the people with whom I have been fortunate to work over the last decade. This includes parishioners, colleagues from the Housing Association world and many friends and fellow travellers from the academic world and elsewhere. I believe that 'our' stories and blurred encounters will illuminate the experiences of a much wider audience and that we might discover that it is worth standing for a while beneath the clock and risking a few brief encounters!

1

Close encounters

This story begins on a summer's evening back in 1987. The doorbell of Lydbury North Vicarage rings. On the doorstep stand a young couple. They have come to see the vicar because they have heard that there is a house in one of our villages that is standing empty. They come from within the immediate locality and they are looking for a property to rent. There is no room for them in their own home country.

They have arrived on my doorstep because they have heard that the church owns this particular property and they imagine that we are going to be able to respond to their need and offer them accommodation. Of course they are going to be disappointed. Things are always more complicated than that. I have to tell them that the house is held in trust, that we are still stuck in fruitless negotiations with the Local Education Authority who have been renting the property but do not want us to rent it out again until we have made a separate entrance to the house away from the school of which it is a part. We have no source of income to pay for this work and so the house remains empty and will continue to deteriorate until somebody comes up with a solution. They leave somewhat downcast. I am equally depressed and ashamed that the local church is apparently unable to exercise its pastoral ministry to care for those in need. Perhaps, for the first time, I see that housing provision really is a pastoral issue. If that was my family in their shoes what would I make of this institution called church that preached one thing and then did the opposite?

This is the beginning of my involvement with the issue of provision of affordable housing and what happened next is recounted in my *Local Theology* (1994). I return to that beginning now because it contrasts so starkly with my current involvement. I want to talk about where this has got to seventeen years later and try to explain to myself why I am now a Board member of Festival Housing Group and part of a Joint Working Group which has recently been investigating the business case for a possible merger with a neighbouring Housing Group. This merger – if it were to have happened – would have resulted in a new group that owned assets worth £330 million, including 12,000 properties, a substantial Care Business owning ten

1

residential care homes, its own Property Care business and also a market rented subsidiary. In the event, the talks were called off after twelve months of negotiations. In addition to this I find myself on the Remuneration Committee of Festival discussing the fine details of payment of Board members after an in-principle decision made by the Board a few months earlier and about which I have severe reservations. All of this has happened because a young couple turned up on my doorstep all that time ago. What am I doing as a parish priest being part of what is effectively a commercial business – albeit one with social objectives – sitting alongside high-flying finance directors let alone our own senior executives who are being paid three or four times more than I am, participating in decisions that are worth sums that I could only dream about?

What I hope will become clear as this story unfolds is that the traditional and familiar boundaries between church and world, between faith and culture if you prefer, are being crossed – and some might say integrities compromised – on an increasingly regular basis. I want to examine why this is happening and to develop ways of evaluating this process. Is there a justification for my presence on the Festival Board, for instance? Now that the housing provision culture in this country has shifted so far towards a commercial base, is it appropriate that the church should be represented in this way or should I rather be on the outside as I was seventeen years ago, criticizing the system and trying to punch holes in it occasionally in order to help individuals in need?

The text will contain a mixture of practical experience and some much more theoretical material. This is quite deliberate and echoes the attempt to construct a contextual theology to be found in *Local Theology*. One of the boundaries that I have found myself crossing is that between theory and practice. Perhaps I no longer hold quite so strictly to the models for this process that I described in that earlier book. The encounters are indeed blurred, although the important ones are certainly not brief, and the blurring is my experience of the way things are at the moment. I hope that others will be able to identify with this feeling as I suspect that those of us who readily engage in social action will share this sense of complexity and confusion. Part of what I want to say is that rather than being a cause for concern this should be a source of encouragement. Blurring is to be expected once we can get a grip on the way that our culture has developed and understand that the familiar divide between reason and all those things that are then sent into the camp of non-reason e.g. faith, needs to be challenged. However, that in itself cannot be enough, for there need to be criteria, or at least ways of judging where and when this blurring is in the service of the Christian tradition within which we stand. At what point is our integrity or our identity compromised by such practical engagements? Is this sometimes what has to happen in order that other things might change and that others may grow – in faith or out of it?

One of my major influences in recent years, the French philosopher Jacques Derrida, not a name frequently encountered in the Housing Association movement, let alone in church circles, has helpfully talked about 'eating well'. I will try to explain this. The fear that Christians often seem to have when they stand on the brink of getting 'involved' in worldly things – not that there is really a choice in the matter – is that of being appropriated by another agenda. The values and practices of the ungodly world 'out there' will start impinging upon the pure and unsullied values and practices of our religious enclave if we allow ourselves to get too close. Politics is a dirty game and economic life is governed by a different set of rules so Christians need to stand aloof and retain a distinct identity. (I call this a 'communitarian' form of Christianity and expressed my criticisms of it in *Beyond All Reason*.) Practical engagement means that we risk being appropriated by this 'alien' world; in Derrida's terms, that we will be 'eaten up by' that other whom we encounter 'out there'. So my question is, can we avoid being 'eaten' if there is to be real encounter? I do not think that we can. I believe that some degree of appropriation is both necessary and inevitable. In which case what is required is the art of 'eating well'! But how do we tell the difference between 'eating well' and getting a severe dose of indigestion? That is the question that I hope to explore in this book.

Church and Welfare

I will return to the Housing Association story in due course, but first I want to offer a series of cameos that illustrate where the relationship between church and welfare stands in this country at the present time. I believe that this is one of the most obvious areas where boundaries have become blurred and where those of us who engage in social action as part of our ministry sometimes wonder quite what we are doing. I will be talking from my experience as a parish priest but also as an Industrial Chaplain. I begin with a flashback in time to the days when the local church was probably the main source of welfare provision in many localities.

In the Four Square parishes in Worcestershire, one of my four parishes, Elmley Lovett, has a trust fund which was set up in the nineteenth century by the then Rector, the Revd Henry Percival, the son of the only British Prime Minister to be shot in the House of Commons, the Honourable Spencer Percival. Henry Percival was a far-sighted individual who realized that the future well-being of the parish and its parishioners might well depend upon owning assets which could not be appropriated by the wider church institution and would be administered from within the parish and only for the benefit of its inhabitants. It would not be appropriate to enter into the details of those assets, but the outcome is that the current trustees – of which the vicar is always chair – may, from time to time and when finances permit, have monies to distribute to three sources. One is to the Parochial Church

Council of the parish, the second is to an Educational Foundation for the benefit of people in the parish, and the third is effectively a Poor Fund to be administered at the vicar's discretion. The latter two create problems for the trustees. The difficulty is always to translate the intentions of the original trust into the present circumstances. There is a Church Voluntary Aided Primary school within the parish with around 95 pupils on roll. This is the obvious beneficiary of the funds from the Educational Foundation. However, as with many small rural primary schools in this area, a significant proportion of the children do not come from within the Four Square parishes, let alone from Elmley Lovett. Many if not all of such local schools survive only because they draw upon a constituency of children from the neighbouring town of Droitwich. Parents want their children to attend schools with smaller class sizes, and sometimes even a church-based ethos, and are wary of some of the town schools. If it were not for this the school in Elmley Lovett would have closed in the 1980s. So children who benefit from the Educational Foundation do not necessarily live within the parish boundaries. However, one can argue that it is the school as an institution which benefits rather than particular individuals and that there would be no school here at all were it not for the presence of children from elsewhere. It is just about possible then to remain within the terms of the original trust.

The Poor Fund however is a different matter. One could argue that this provision predates the creation of the Welfare State and was part of the local church's contribution to local welfare provision – perhaps all that there was in any institutional sense in those days. Now of course the state has taken over that role – although as we know that is changing as we speak – and there is a stigma attached to receiving 'welfare' or 'hand-outs' from any source, be it state or church. If there are individuals who qualify for such provision it is unlikely that they would be prepared to openly admit it, or even to come to the vicar privately. The result of this is that we have monies that accumulate but with no obvious beneficiaries. The only course of action is for the trustees to argue a case with the Charity Commissioners to redefine the terms of this part of the trust, having first established that there are no calls upon it.

I tell this story because it both illustrates the way in which the church was involved in welfare provision before the advent of the Welfare State and also raises questions about what may yet happen as current approaches to government provision of welfare come under threat. Even though such trusts appear to have become redundant in areas with a reasonable degree of affluence, any of us engaged in large scale fund-raising activities know how significant some of the larger trust funds are as an alternative source of capital and one wonders whether even such locally-based trusts as the one described may not again, one day soon, play a larger role in welfare provision. If the Welfare State comes and then goes, it throws institutions such as the church back into the fray.

In fact, one can begin to see that this is already starting to happen. The examples that I will now offer make it clear that the church – or rather "faith communities" – are now seen as increasingly significant 'partners' by the government. I have placed those terms in inverted commas quite deliberately because they both rest upon certain assumptions that require careful scrutiny. I will register my reservations now although I want to return to them in more detail at later stages.

To describe religious groupings as 'faith communities' is to accept the very division between faith and reason that I want to bring into question. Briefly, it suggests that religion is largely, if not exclusively, a matter of faith, in other words, it is subjective, related to the emotional, not capable of becoming engaged in 'rational' or public debate and that other 'communities', those of business, commerce or politics are, by contrast, objective, autonomous and governed by open and rational processes of discussion and negotiation. I hope to show that these descriptions are both unhelpful and inaccurate and that they characterize contemporary culture in ways that are damaging to public life. As for the use of the term 'partner', this has become the fashionable 'political-speak' for drawing both private enterprise and voluntary bodies, such as churches, back into the ambit of government, particularly when it comes to financing major projects or providing resources of people and time. In fact it encompasses a variety of relationships between the different 'partners' and is one of the major reasons for the blurring of encounters that I intend to examine. It is a 'catch-all' term that begs all the key questions about the exact nature of the relationships. When is a partner not a partner? Does a true partnership require a 50–50 split of power and responsibility? Who is eating whom and with what degree of satisfaction? There is much here that needs to be questioned.

Local Strategic Partnerships

For those not yet familiar with this recent item of government terminology LSPs form a key component of attempts to revitalize and regenerate neighbourhoods – well, there is another question, because one immediately runs into a further set of terms that are part of the same policy package. We are called upon to renew and regenerate 'neighbourhoods', but what exactly is the definition of 'neighbourhood'? We all now know that we do not know what we mean by 'community' although the term continues to be used, so the focus is switched to neighbourhoods instead. We all live in neighbourhoods, even though these may not form communities in any identifiable sense. I am not sure that this really succeeds in getting the debate any further. Presumably, to adopt a lowest common denominator approach, it merely means that people live in close proximity to other people, i.e. neighbours, and that if you put enough of these together in one locality it then forms a 'neighbourhood'! Ignoring, for the sake of argument, the fact that some people live very geographi-cally isolated lives, it must presuppose that those who live in close proximity have something in common with one another, although it is not immediately obvious what that might be. Perhaps it is purely and simply geographical proximity. However, let us just accept that this is part of the discourse now used when dealing with government agencies.

How effective such LSPs might be and exactly how they operate seems to depend upon where you are in the country. That is not the issue that concerns me here. It is the role of faith communities within LSPs that is of real interest. Let us examine a recent booklet produced jointly by the New Economics Foundation and the Church Urban Fund entitled *Faith, Hope and Participation* (2001). It helpfully provides some definitions and explanations.

It has been recognized that many recent initiatives such as City Challenge and the Single Regeneration Budget have not delivered what was hoped for but instead lead to further waves of apathy and disillusion. 'Areas selected for regeneration were sometimes so large that they often ended up excluding the experience of local people' (p. 6). What is now required then is that local people claim ownership of such projects. This has led to the National Strategy for Neighbourhood Renewal which was published by the Social Exclusion Unit in January 2001, focusing attention on community empowerment and authentic ownership by local people. LSPs are 'the key vehicle for leading and implementing neighbourhood renewal' bringing together the public, private, voluntary and community sectors in a 'single, overarching, local co-ordination framework' (p. 7). Local Authority boundaries are often the geographical determinants of the LSPs. Their tasks, as determined by the government are to enable effective community participation; to access resources within the community that cannot normally be tapped by the statutory sector; to try to reach the parts of communities that others have failed to reach and to develop mechanisms to secure the genuine involvement of all sectors of the local community.

It is obvious that faith communities will be seen to be a vital component of this strategy, forming one of the sectors that bring people together for common activity. This booklet defines such communities as 'a specific group of people who live in a particular neighbourhood and belong to a certain religious tradition' (p. 9). It goes on to suggest that these groups have a particular contribution to make because of their transformative capacity: 'breathing life into the dead bones of housing estates; continuing to hope in the unlikeliest of circumstances; not giving up on people; believing people can re-create' (p. 9). Beyond this, they also contribute to creating a sense of identity, offering care and support to those in need, exercising a prophetic ministry and providing essential local spaces and infrastructure. Examples are then offered to support these conclusions.

All of this is inspiring and encouraging and indeed pays tribute to what local faith communities are capable of doing at their best, given the appropriate resources and motivation. This would indeed mean that they would be an important way of gaining access to local people and encouraging participation in renewal initiatives. However, as has been pointed out (Atherton 2003), it is invariably struggling and marginalized church communities who are being called upon by LSPs to supplement welfare provision in deprived areas. It is where resources are already stretched to the limit and beyond that more pressure is being placed to deliver even more. I also question whether there are these hidden and inaccessible communities beneath the surface that the government strategy presupposes. Who is actually going to 'deliver the goods' of neighbourhood renewal beyond the already stretched religious groupings? Is this merely yet another slice of government rhetoric designed to appear to address the consequences of social exclusion by shifting the responsibility of welfare provision back to the voluntary sector and particularly to such faith communities? Where is the 'partnership' in this unless root causes of marginalization are addressed and new central resources are allocated to assist in this process?

For local religious groupings however it is difficult to resist such overtures for local involvement. For those faith communities that already see their ministry in this way it sounds like an acknowledgement and recognition of the role that they play and maybe even the promise of more resources. It is also a way of feeling that one can make a real difference by tapping into the structures of local and national government. Crucially, it appears to offer the promise of being allowed to play a more substantial role in public life and of gaining a place and a voice at the tables of power. The approaches are seductive to the point of being irresistible. But whose agenda is dominant in this? Who is appropriating whom and who is really 'eating well' in this process? Here is the dilemma which faith communities always face. If we choose to remain aloof and not get involved, forever suspicious and critical of the agendas of the statutory authorities, we stand convicted of missing opportunities for both prophetic and pastoral ministry. If we do get involved, we run the risk of being consumed or compromised by somebody else's agenda. How might we retain our identity and integrity within all of this? In the end, does this matter?

One must be alert to the agenda of central government and to the assumptions about matters of faith that lie behind it. One of the major drivers is indeed an unwillingness by successive governments to take the political risk of funding welfare provision through higher (direct) taxation. Thus, alternative providers of welfare need to be identified. Voluntary groups are the obvious alternative – perhaps we will need more Henry Percivals again in the near future! This is a major problem facing all Western economies given the ageing population, increasing levels of dependency, pressures upon pensions and so on. However, there is also an assumption in this that faith communities operate in what I have already referred to earlier as a 'communitarian' fashion. In other words, they form tight-knit and potentially exclusive groupings based upon clear boundaries and a common identity and shared values. Only if this is the case are they capable of 'delivering' the alternative welfare provision and access to community resources required by LSPs. I would want to question this both in terms of practice and of theory. What concerns me about this approach is that it assumes a closed or exclusive sense of identity when I believe that what should and will be happening where religious groups respond to the challenges of economic and cultural change is the construction of open and inclusive identities.

I think it is valuable to get an outsider's perspective on where and how local churches are realistically expected to make an impact upon public life within a particular locality. I want to refer to a recent document published by the National Housing Federation called *Regional Futures and Neighbourhood Realities* (Scase and Scales 2003). This forms part of an agenda by the National Housing Federation to improve its public profile and thus that of Housing Associations generally, but the document is valuable in its own right as it offers projections into the future on a whole range of social changes. Its penultimate chapter paints a series of scenarios of different places and communities as they might well look by the year 2010. Amongst these are a northern town, on the edge of a large scale conurbation and suffering from the effects of loss of manufacturing industry, full-time employment and so on; an isolated Cornish village; a deprived inner London borough and an ethnically diverse town in the East Midlands highly dependent upon new technologies and improved transport infrastructure. Does the church get a mention in any of these? The one location where church is described as playing any sort of a role is in a market town not far from Cambridge with an ageing population. In this locality:

> Neighbourhood commitment is high. The local church is seen to symbolize its heart and soul and many of the church attendees are not so much religious as dedicated members of the neighbourhood. It is around the church that many of the wide-ranging voluntary organizations are established. It is through these that the local population is mobilized when there are any rumours suggesting that the status quo could be under threat. For example, it was particularly vocal against the proposal to expand Stansted airport in 2005 and, more recently, there was a proposal from the County Council that the town should absorb the construction of 500 executive homes to respond to the population pressures of East Anglia. (p. 82)

Now I accept that this is no more than the projections made by two individuals, albeit they are based on genuine research e.g. the British Household Panel Survey, but I think it is interesting that no faith community appears in the scenarios where LSPs currently might want them to operate. Where the church does appear it is essentially conservative (and probably 'Conservative' as well), providing voluntary activity for and by an ageing population and fighting for the status quo. In other words, what is left is exactly a 'communitarian' church based upon a monochrome social grouping and what appears to be a closed or exclusive identity. So this is the limit of the public influence of what remains of religious groupings in a few years' time and the idea that there are vibrant, active and critically-motivated faith communities operating in areas of deprivation and social exclusion contributing to the renewal of neighbourhoods does not appear.

Perhaps it would be a mistake to read too much into this. After all it is not an officially government sponsored document and is targeted towards Housing Associations and their growing role in neighbourhood renewal. However, as an external perception of what religious groups really are and might offer to public life in the near future, it is fairly disturbing. It might be correct of course. Churches might only survive in the comfortable enclaves of Middle England. Other faith communities could still be present in other locations, but only as those tight-knit groupings preserving a religious or cultural identity increasingly under threat from the surrounding culture. If this were to be the true expectation of officialdom of the future of institutional religion in this country, then the rhetoric of LSPs and of neighbourhood renewal would have to be seen in a different light. We are useful for as long as we happen to survive, but are of no real interest or concern to government in our own right. We are just a convenient and temporary vehicle for the delivery of alternative welfare, and even much of that is probably a smokescreen for deeper political agendas!

Church and Commerce

Another area where the boundaries are blurred is that of the churches' relationship to the commercial world. I write this from the background of being an Industrial Chaplain with the specific brief of trying to make connections between the churches and the worlds of commerce and industry. In the early days of Industrial Mission the clear objective was to establish a presence within large scale manufacturing plants and to carry the mission of the church out to ordinary working people who might not otherwise encounter the Christian Gospel. The days of large scale manufacturing plants, of steel works, shipyards, volume motor car building and the carpet manufacturing which was the original base for the Industrial Mission team in Kidderminster where I am located, are long gone. If the primary means of spreading the Gospel is to encounter as many people at work as one can, then one needs to visit the offices of Local Authorities, or be involved in Local Primary Care Trusts, or even Housing Associations and Universities. Such are often the major employers in many of our cities and towns. A further development of Industrial Mission is into the sphere of retail chaplaincy where major new shopping complexes such as the MetroCentre in Gateshead or Bluewater in Kent now have their own full-time chaplains ministering to management, staff and customers. It seems to me that the exact objective of this ministry has always been somewhat blurred. For instance, the Ford Motor Company, with a number of plants in the West Midlands, has recently been courting Industrial Mission, even being prepared to make a financial contribution towards the project of getting a chaplain on site. However, they do not appear to have one agreed objective for this work. One plant sees it very much in terms of offering a counselling service to employees. Another plant was looking for somebody to be present on the shop floor in order to pick up any issues or concerns that could then be fed back to senior management. Both appear to serve the purposes of the management team in a very particular way. Most Industrial Chaplains themselves appear to view the task as partly pastoral – just being around and creating relationships of trust over time in case individuals should wish to share confidential, personal problems, so quite similar to parish life – and partly as direct engagement with local economic life so as better to act as a channel of communication and interpretation between the church and the world. This might mean exercising a prophetic ministry at some point, or acting in an advocacy role in certain situations, but always aware that one is a guest in a working environment where it is easily possible to outstay one's welcome. Hence the role is explicitly that of crossing boundaries with all the inherent ambiguities that involves.

Another aspect of this work is the role of churches within town centres, clearly crossing the boundary back into parish life. As part of my particular responsibility I have been working with the Baxter Church in Kidderminster (URC) to see if they could make a more effective use of their substantial church building and plant in the middle of the town and close to a new shopping development. This led to visits to a number of other town centre churches or ecumenical centres to see what models of engagement they had been able to establish. Although each of these proved to be quite different, they all seemed to face the difficult question of whether they were essentially housing voluntary activities or engaging directly in commercial business.

For instance, the idea of having a coffee shop and indeed a Christian bookshop was initially attractive to the Baxter Church project because a number of other churches had gone down that road. However, when we examined these in more detail some ambiguities emerged. Some of the coffee shops were run totally by volunteers, catering for people who would not be able to pay large amounts towards food and drink, and effectively being a drop-in centre for those who needed to come into town centres for public life and company. Not being in the business of making money they require subsidy from one source or another. Other coffee shops however were being run on commercial lines, with professionally trained staff and sometimes with the business being sub-contracted to a firm which then took all the financial risks and responsibilities. These were less about providing a service to those in need and more about generating income. The ecumenical centres in Telford and Milton Keynes house large-scale voluntary operations, some of them directly church-based and others not and tap into sources of government funding towards training of young people.

The Crossing Centre in St Paul's Church in the centre of Walsall is a particularly interesting development quite unlike any other that we visited. On entering what appears to be the shell of a rather dour and forbidding church building at the back of the bus station one walks straight into a small shopping mall with attractive and brightly-lit small shop units. In one corner of the ground floor is a chapel which is used for midweek services and there is a nursery facility towards the back of the building. On the first floor is a large worship area, with considerable flexibility and good sound equipment and then some office space and a large commercially run coffee shop and meeting area. The second floor is mostly taken up with conference rooms and more office space including that of the manager of the centre. The whole project took a considerable time to come to fruition, was part-funded by the Diocese of Lichfield and is still facing questions of financial viability. There is no question that current financial circumstances in the Church of England would preclude contributions towards such a project in the future. The main source of income generation is the letting of the conference facilities and the in-house catering for those. However, this is a commercial business and one where the competition is fierce. The shop units and the coffee shop itself do not subsidize the running costs of the building. The vision behind the project is commendable and exciting but, as a viable commercial enterprise it appears to be a failure. This is in contrast to the ecumenical centre in Swindon, where the coffee shop is effectively a drop-in centre with a small interview room for private consultation, plus a worship centre and some office space on the first floor and where the finances seemed to be a mystery. However, this is possibly because the original church building, of which this is one section only, is leased out to commercial businesses and so the church operation is subsidized by substantial rental income.

As I said, there is no one model in operation here, and different historical circumstances and financial possibilities mean that each project is unique and impossible to replicate. The basic tension is between operating a commercial enterprise and a voluntary group facility. It is possible to do both with an element of cross-subsidy, but then that means that the outreach work is constantly vulnerable to changing financial circumstances. As many of us know from within the voluntary sector itself, one of the key questions now being posed to new projects is that of sustainability. It is not just a matter of getting capital funding to establish a worthy or high profile project but of working out how that project is going to be sustained over time. Can it generate its own income at an appropriate level or will it 'go out of business' once the initial grants and indeed enthusiasm run out? One thing that churches find hard to accept is that in the harsh environment of the commercial world, businesses come and go with disturbing rapidity. Everything is 'for the time being' only and it is to be expected that such enterprises will have a very limited life span. In the churches we tend to plan for the longer term, hoping that people's voluntary contributions, either financial or in terms of time, will be repaid by the sustainability of the projects we establish. Perhaps one of the boundaries we are being challenged to cross is that of accepting that many of our church projects have to be 'for the time being' only and that our good intentions cannot be translated into long term benefits.

Is this though to allow ourselves to become subject to the modus operandi and the ethos of a commercial culture that we should in fact be challenging and to which religious communities should be offering an alternative? Are Christians allowing themselves to be appropriated and their integrity and identities compromised by getting so close to the business world? How can we judge the difference between 'service to the world' and 'subservience to the world'? Are we able to keep alive the alternatives which we believe are central to the Christian message when we get as involved as Industrial Mission or retail chaplaincy are accustomed to do or are we simply singing from somebody else's hymn sheet? These are some of the questions that I want to address.

The Concept of Social Enterprise

I think it is worth offering a similar example from the field of the voluntary sector. As already mentioned one of the key problems with many community based activities is that of sustainability. Although it may well be possible to identify sources of capital funding to cover the initial outlay for any new project, it is assumed that such projects will have to find ways of generating their own income if they are to be sustained. The concept of social enterprise appears to have been coined in order to encourage the voluntary sector to do just this. I refer here to the document produced by the National Council for Voluntary Organisations, *What is Social Enterprise*, once again produced in partnership with the New Economics Foundation and available on their website.

So, what is social enterprise? It means that a group or organization is trading for a social purpose. This can happen in a number of ways. It could mean that the product is social, so, for instance, a neighbourhood nursery, a credit union or fresh food cooperative trading where previously such facilities did not exist. It could mean that the processes involved in the trading serve a social purpose. In others words creating employment or training opportunities or perhaps embedding fair trade within the means of production. Finally, of course, the profits made could be used for social purposes. Charity shops are an obvious example of this. This raises interesting questions about a whole series of enterprises and whether or not they fall into this category. It certainly represents a blurring of the boundaries between the voluntary sector and commercial activity. One wonders whether this is really a partnership between quite different sets of values and ways of operating or whether it is the take-over of the voluntary sector by a business ethic. There will probably be no one answer to this as different projects will be placed at different points along a spectrum.

It is interesting to read the language that is used in the document from the NCVO. For instance 'at the heart of social enterprise lies the concept of the double (or triple to include the environmental) bottom line'. It reminds me of a conversation that happened within Festival Housing Group about the idea of 'Pastoral Accounting'. Clearly the idea is that the particular organization has targets and aspirations that cannot simply be measured in financial terms. So, for instance, other social objectives are built into the corporate plans. This is all very fine in theory, but I always worry about which set of objectives are given priority when the pressure is really on and potential financial commitments or losses are at stake! That is why I worry about the introduction of what are in fact conflicting values into the voluntary sector. Once again it is matter of appropriation or of 'eating well'.

However, having said that, it is clear that this is one way forward for voluntary projects during times of financial stringency and where on-going support for such activities cannot be guaranteed. While researching possible models for the Baxter Church project we visited a fascinating project in Oswestry called the Qube. It has been set up in a building in the centre of the town as a base for a number of the local voluntary groups, for instance, the voluntary car scheme, but has been based around an Arts project and so includes a small art gallery and a workshop where art activity can take place. There are also offices and other community space, although both have obviously been given a lower priority than the arts activities. Something like £350,000 of public grant funding has gone into this in order to convert the building. It also includes an ICT (Information, Communications Technology) suite used in partnership with the local college. It is very impressive and indeed looks good. However, the unanswered question, we felt, was that of sustainability. How was this project going to be able to generate income to support its on-going work? Is this yet another example of the disturbing government policy of creating lots of high-profile projects which allow them to claim fairly instant success, but in fact have no real prospect of long-term viability? One cannot tell from a brief visit, but there are clearly questions there for the future.

As far as the NCVO is concerned, the concept of social enterprise is an exciting one that augers a better future for the voluntary sector. 'At its most exciting, social enterprise is a means of allocating wealth and resources on a social basis that steers a steady path between the fallacy of free market trickle down, the limits of "charity" and the discredited appeal of a centrally controlled economy'. One can see the attraction of such an idea, but I do wonder whether this is to claim a bit too much. It is less a means of overturning the current economic system and offering a viable large-scale alternative to it than about learning to operate pragmatically within the existing system and perhaps presenting projects in a way that might encourage other sources of partnership funding. That may be no bad thing in itself, but it is perhaps slightly less revolutionary than the rhetoric appears to be claiming.

The Voluntary and the Professional

I want to return now to my first example and mention something significant that is happening in the Housing Association movement. The payment of Board members has been discussed within the movement for quite a while, but it has now reached the stage where a formal consultation document has been produced and all Housing Associations are taking a view on whether or not this is a path they wish to pursue. Festival Housing Group has made an in-principle decision to pay Board members – although the detail of this is still being negotiated as I write – and I am part of the working group looking at this. Apparently about one third of Housing Associations have made the same decision, another third are waiting to see what happens with those, and the final third have decided not to pursue this option. The arguments for and against are interesting and complex and I will not go into the finer details here. However, it is clearly another instance of the crossing or blurring of boundaries. Board members, up until this point, have been volunteers, receiving only their travelling expenses at best. The fear is that payment will lead to a change of ethos within the organizations involved and within the movement generally. On a purely personal level, I did not become a Board member in order to receive tenants' money to compensate me for the time that I give. That is the only source of funding that we as an organization have and I do not like to think that we would have to sacrifice building another property in order to pay Board members. However, there are arguments on the other side about the increased demands that are now made upon members and the levels of financial responsibility that they carry and therefore standards and qualities of professional expertise that are required. All of this I can duly acknowledge. The role is a demanding one and requires a substantial time commitment, particularly from Chairs of Boards. One can see that some level of compensation for this may not be entirely unreasonable. It is also argued that this will lead to improved levels of governance and the possibility of Board members being appraised in that role and therefore ceasing to carry it out if they do not perform effectively.

What concerns me is the motivation for becoming a Board member once payment becomes the reward. Will there be people wanting to do it only because they are receiving payment for it? If a decision is made only to pay Chairs of Boards – which it is possible to do – what tensions and power struggles will it lead to within Boards? Will there be first and second class Board members? If the task is becoming so professionalized – because that is the real message that is being given out in this debate – who will feel qualified or confident enough to take on these roles, other perhaps than other housing professionals or accountants? In which case, what happens to the ethos of community representation and especially tenant representation on Boards? What appears to be happening is that the role of Board members is subtly evolving into a more professionalized set of tasks, very often the management of finances and personnel, and this could happen at the expense of the social and community functions of the business. Are Housing Associations a classic instance of social enterprise as previously defined? Is the product social? One could argue that it is, assuming that the main objective is the provision of affordable housing , although many have now diversified into other areas, some of them more commercially orientated. The process may be social, but probably only incidentally through the provision of training opportunities for apprentices for instance. The profit is certainly meant to be social as we exist to make surpluses that can then be fed back into the organization towards further development. So we do appear to be a social enterprise. However, we are also operating within a competitive environment where we compete against other Housing Associations for development grant and options on building land let alone for key staff and other scarce resources. Hence we are a strange hybrid of social action for the benefit of others and big business where financial constraints and criteria are paramount. Our boundaries are inherently blurred.

It needs to be said that the same is increasingly true for other public bodies, notably Health Care Trusts and indeed school governors. For the latter there is now yet another government attempt to reconstitute governing bodies which will probably lead to a streamlining and reduction of numbers of governors and thus the need to recruit people with the appropriate professional skills, educational, financial, legal and those who deal with public premises. Since a proportion of these have to be parents one does wonder how some communities are going to be able to fill these positions. Once again the requirements are increasing and the recruitment of governors is likely to become more difficult. The task is becoming professionalized. What then are we to make of this general movement?

From Practice to Theory

I hope that this series of cameos has shown how the boundaries are becoming more blurred and how new questions are arising, particularly for socially engaged churches and their members. What we now require is a framework which helps us to understand what is happening and to try to identify ways of evaluating where and when these processes are acceptable for those of us within the Christian tradition. This final section is no more than the beginning of this.

As I was writing this I was reminded of a concept that I first encountered back in the 1980s, one which was coined by another of my theoretically-based influences, the philosopher and sociologist Habermas. As part of his wider theory of contemporary society and his attempt to develop a critical perspective on the developments of capitalism he came up with the notion of the 'colonization of the lifeworld'. My own halting interpretation of this is that he is pointing to an increased tendency of the values and structures of what he calls the Systems World – the way in which big business and commerce operate – to invade or encroach upon areas of our lives that have previously been determined by different values, especially those associated with community and relationships. As this theory forms part of a much more complex series of ideas that I want to talk about in the next chapter I merely want to offer clues to its possible use at this stage.

One could argue that each of the examples I have given do indeed point towards this tendency of the business world and its values to appropriate the territory of churches, voluntary groups and charitable organizations. This may be disguised underneath the language of partnership and all the government rhetoric about creating sustainable communities and more effective governance, but this is what is really happening. So how can these other groups retain their distinctive values and ideals, some of which may be in direct contradiction to the Systems World that is now moving in on them? Is this a matter of 'eating well' or of being consumed to the point of extinction? I think it is important to guard against two extreme interpretations of what is going on.

Why is this process occurring at all? One possible explanation is that in the 'good old days' – if they ever existed – when this country was largely under the influence of Christian values and there was some sort of social consensus over what were acceptable forms of behaviour and the conduct of public life, it was much easier to create a type of social conscience where those who had (wealth) might be encouraged to contribute towards the needs of those who did not. However, that situation no longer holds as we encounter a series or plurality of different value systems and the political correctness of our time determines that no one of these should be paramount over the others. Hence there is a fragmentation of public life and consequently the necessary processes of negotiation between conflicting value systems. Within that sort of structure there is always the danger of creating a vacuum into which the 'lowest common denominator' of public life readily leaps. That lowest common denominator is money. It is access to financial resources which now becomes the determining factor even in areas that previously played by different rules, those of community, family and religion. So what we have are two competing and opposed value systems, one claiming to operate in terms of reason, neutral accounting processes and a high level of objectivity. When agreement between the other value systems, those based on historical tradition and even myth, feelings, ritual and all things subjective becomes impossible, the only way of dealing with the problem of allocating scarce resources is to resort to the supposedly safe financial criteria. These two worlds – the lifeworld and the Systems World – collide, and there can only ever be one winner. That is one extreme interpretation of what is happening.

The other extreme is to say that what this actually represents is the breakdown of the Systems World under the pressures of its own internal contradictions. This way of working cannot be sustained for long simply because it is incapable of doing justice to or acknowledging the importance in people's lives of those other human values that are just as essential for personal and community life. In fact what is going on through this blurring of boundaries, it is argued, is the beginning of the resurgence of those alternative values. Government welfare provision, for instance, has recognized that it cannot cope without drawing in the resources of faith communities. This is the beginning of a turn-around in which the world that had been 'disenchanted' and lost its sense of a deeper meaning is being 're-enchanted' and those former values and religious structures will once again come to the fore.

This is to present the debate as a battle between good and evil, between darkness and light – always much easier to grasp and to offer one a clear sense of identity. However, I do not believe that either of these extremes do justice to present realities. I want to argue that this way of construing the relationship between faith and, let us call it reason, is inaccurate or unhelpful, and that what the blurring of boundaries should point us towards is a new and developing relationship between these two, one that has yet to fully emerge but that requires great attention and dedication. This will demand that I now give some space to the theoretical resources, but, in the midst of this, I do not want to lose sight of where this story began, the couple on my doorstep looking for a place to live. They must be the final test of whatever theories and practices we develop.

2

Of the third kind

Encountering the Other

A few months ago there was a bad accident on one of the nearby motorways. It so happened that a member of St John Ambulance was travelling in a vehicle that was caught up in this event. As he got out of his car to see what was going on and if he could offer assistance a nurse in uniform got out of another car and was about to come over to the scene of the crash. He looked at her and then pointed out that if she was going to get involved she needed to put a coat on over her uniform, otherwise she could be deemed to be attending the incident in an official capacity. Health service staff are now warned against getting involved in any incident in an unofficial capacity because they are making themselves liable to be sued for negligence should anything go wrong. Gone are the days when you could expect the announcement 'Is there a doctor in the house?' to yield any response. I mention this as it is a contemporary example of the way in which the familiar moral imperative to help another person in need is being undermined by what is called the litigation culture. Perhaps the story has echoes of the parable of the Good Samaritan.

The theme of encountering the other and then responding to them – assuming that the other is a person of course – is deeply embedded in the Christian tradition and indeed in many other religions. It is also a key part of the developing philosophy that, for convenience only, I will refer to as postmodern. Although it is the philosophical dimension that I will concentrate upon in this chapter, I want first to offer a human angle on the debate and relate the ideas to more familiar religious territory.

From the strand of the Old Testament known as the Deuteronomic tradition, there is a clear directive that the children of Israel are to offer care to the alien, the fatherless and the widow (Deut. 10: 18–20). This is important because God cared for his people when they were in need and it is incumbent upon them to do the same for others. It may well be that this is expressed in terms of particular categories of 'others', but the principle is clear. Within the New Testament one encounters the same message. The famous passage from St Matthew chapter 25 tells us that

19

whenever we meet somebody else who is in need then we are in fact encountering Christ and should respond accordingly. 'Whatever you do for one of the least of these, you do it for me'. In addition, as already mentioned, the Parable of the Good Samaritan is probably the most famous example of the same directive (Luke 10: 25–37). The story is told to answer the question 'And who is my neighbour?' Jesus makes it plain that my neighbour is anybody in need, whatever creed, race or colour. So encountering 'the other', invariably calls forth from us a response of care and concern, especially when that other person is in difficulties.

However, this theme of responding to 'the other' has now become one of the touchstones of postmodern philosophy. Once again, I want to draw only brief attention to this before moving into the more detailed exposition. There are a number of different candidates for 'the other'. If one concentrates upon feminist writing then it is either male or female who are 'the other'. This is the key or defining difference according to the most extreme interpretations. The 'other' is a person of the other gender and it is this sexual difference that determines the nature of human encounter. Other differences are clearly possible, including those of race and nationality, and there are those who would argue that it is these that most urgently require our attention. There is also the 'other' that is the natural world, that which is not humanity, and relationships between the human and the non-human are often a focus for the theories behind environmental movements. From within the field of psychology there is Jung's idea of the Shadow side and Freud's notion of the unconscious, the 'other' within each one of us that is always likely to shape our feelings and identity in ways of which we are unaware. So there are both internal and external 'others'. Finally, there is the idea of God as 'wholly other', that which is so different from all human being that it eludes our conceptual grasp completely and is beyond both articulation and comprehension. It would seem that as soon as one identifies oneself according to some description or set of characteristics there is automatically an 'other' of one sort or another, that which is different and even unacknowledged. One is then faced with the question of the extent and significance of these differences. Is the 'other' so different as to remain beyond the scope of normal encounter and relationship and exactly how far is one to carry this moral imperative to respond to the other in need? Do we even begin to understand the complexity of human – and other – relationships without some deeper insight into the nature of our differences and the extent of our similarities? As soon as we use language and concepts we are caught up in this inevitable tension between identity and difference, between that which is and that which is not. This area of exploration of the nature and quality of relationships, both personal and non-personal, is crucial for the subject of blurring boundaries and interpreting contemporary culture.

Faith as the 'other' of reason

In the previous chapter I described a series of contemporary encounters which make it clear that the territory of faith and that of public life, business and commerce are seen as separate and distinct worlds. The very use of the term 'faith community' current in both political and religious discourses suggests that there is something about such groupings which sets them apart from other aspects of contemporary society. 'Faith' – whatever that is – is not to be found, presumably, in non-religious areas of our lives, otherwise there would be no point in using the term to describe these groupings. Put in such a stark manner, one may immediately begin to doubt that areas of human activity are quite so clear-cut and indeed, it is exactly this assumption that I will be challenging shortly. However, the assumption is now so common and so deeply embedded in our culture to the point where even 'faith communities' themselves accept it, that we need to understand how this has come about. In order to do this I need to tell the currently accepted story of the separation of faith from reason.

It is not possible to go into this account in great detail, so what I offer here is the briefest of outlines. Along with many others over the years I have attempted to work through this narrative in greater depth (Reader 2002), but this must be a thumbnail sketch only.

The story normally begins with the Enlightenment. Much could be said about this including highlighting the danger of constructing the Enlightenment as a monochrome and coherent movement of thought created by certain key individuals as a deliberate and sustained attack upon religion. There are good reasons to challenge this view of what was much more of a patchwork of ideas and suggestions that built up over a period of time and often contained an ambivalent rather than automatically hostile approach to religion. However, it is always easier to tell a story with a simpler focus, and so the account that has become the conventional wisdom tells us that the Enlightenment was an attempt to break away from the stifling influence of religious ideas and structures in order to free human beings to think for themselves. Rather than accepting certain truths on the authority of a religious tradition on the basis that they had been revealed, for instance through the person of Jesus Christ, humans are now challenged to work matters out for themselves using only their powers of reasoning. The only authority to be accepted is that of what can be directly experienced, described, quantified and codified. Hence the developing role of scientific thought eventually becomes the complete antithesis of the realm of faith which is now seen to be based purely upon myth and superstition.

As I have said, this is more of a caricature than an accurate account of a complex and subtle series of intellectual developments. Certainly a closer study of the work of Kant, deemed to be one of the founding fathers of the Enlightenment, will reveal a rather different picture. His intentions were not to downgrade religion,

but to place it on a sounder footing, one which was based upon a clear demarcation between what reason could be expected to deliver and what could 'reasonably'
be contained in the sphere of religion. The details of this are themselves complex
given that Kant himself talked about different types of reason and different types
of religion, but what is significant now is not what he actually said, but the impact
his work has had on the wider debate. What emerged from this work was a power
struggle between faith and reason where the latter began to dictate to the former
exactly where it was to be located in the realms of culture and intellectual thought.
So it was not that religion was dismissed as of no significance, but rather that it
found itself becoming subject to another train or tradition of thought that exercised
an increasing independence. It represented a shift of power within the relationship,
perhaps even the wayward teenager stretching her wings and deciding for herself
what to believe and how to act. Humanity was starting to grow up and to leave
behind the strictures of the rather stuffy parent otherwise known as Christianity.

The effect of this movement, in the longer term, was to create a rift between
faith and reason and even to question whether there could still be a relationship
between them. It is the implications of this cultural divide that were encountered
in the opening chapter. From a Christian perspective this has led to a series of
different reactions over the last 250 years. One extreme position is to accept that
the two represent totally opposed and alien orders and to maintain that faith has its
own truth and validity that cannot be measured or described except within its own
clear boundaries. Gospel and culture stand on mountain tops facing each other and
occasionally shouting across using words that the other cannot understand. Truth is
only that which has been revealed through the sources of the Christian faith, notably
Scripture, and no external criteria of interpretation can be granted any validity.
The Christian faith community is self-contained, referring only to its own internal
sources of authority and possessing its own unique and distinctive approaches to
all areas of human life, e.g. the family, economics, culture and even politics. To
engage directly with the worldly versions of all of these is to risk contaminating
and compromising the purity of the faith. Or, if there is to be engagement it can
only be on terms dictated by the Christian tradition and subject to its criteria of
interpretation.

In many ways this extreme approach then lets the rest of contemporary culture
off the hook as it can simply go on its own way regardless, convinced that it has
no need to take account of the views and ideas of such an idiosyncratic tradition.
The two worlds may collide occasionally, but only to be in conflict. So the arenas
of science, commerce and politics operate by a different set of rules determined
by an elusive notion of reason and need have no serious contact with the arena of
faith which appears to have much more of the subjective, the emotional and the
authoritarian about it. Hence the contemporary rift between Christianity and public

life: they are simply different worlds! Various versions of this theological approach have been developed over the years, ranging from the reaction of Karl Barth to the liberal Protestantism leading up to the First World War to the recent emergence of radical orthodoxy and its assumption that Christianity can once again present itself as a Grand Narrative now that postmodernity has undermined the claims of reason (Reader 1997).

However, this could be accused of being a somewhat one-sided account and so one needs to acknowledge the difficulties encountered by the other obvious approach. Rather than accepting the assumption that there can be no relationship between reason and faith, the alternative is to try to engage the two on some sort of neutral territory. Once again there have been high profile theologians who have pursued this route. When I was a student in the 1970s the names of Tillich, Bultmann, Niebuhr and Pannenberg were to the fore. Since then the debates have moved on and much recent theology has been influenced by feminist and environmental thinking. The accusation that is always levelled at such approaches is that this is to allow the world to set the agenda and to collude with values and principles that are alien to the Christian tradition. The danger of this is that Christians may become blinded to the evils of contemporary politics and culture to the point where they are appropriated by it and fail to resist when resistance is called for – hence Barth's reaction to the churches' failure to oppose authoritarian regimes. One is either for or against and there can be no middle way. To attempt to engage with the forces of reason is now to fall into the trap of believing that there can be a safe and justifiable middle way. The examples examined in the opening chapter would all fall under this condemnation according to this accusation. The worlds of faith and reason must be kept apart: each is the other's 'other'.

A further implication of accepting this assumption is that the world of faith is then all too readily identified with all the other 'others' of reason, the irrational, the subjective, the affective or emotional dimensions of human subjectivity, the unconscious, the private and domestic and that which is always beyond articulation. As a result it can have no engagement with the areas of life now determined by its 'other', reason, for instance the worlds of politics, economics, science, public morality, business and commerce and even education and academia. It is my belief that this cultural split – one might almost describe it as a form of schizophrenia – is deeply embedded in both religion and culture, is highly damaging to both and now needs to be re-examined and re-described. How is 'faith' to relate to its 'other', reason? If a way cannot be found then neither side can claim any degree of self-awareness or hope for the new beginnings which they claim to promote. I will now suggest a possible way forward.

The art of 'deconstruction'

What we are searching for now is the possibility of other relationships between faith and reason. Rather than simply rejecting all that is put under the heading of Enlightenment and risk reverting to an earlier time and set of assumptions I want to move the debate forward. I will now offer a lengthy quotation to support my argument that I am not alone in this project but can claim allies from amongst members of the philosophical community. This comes from a book that was written following a conference on the subject of where and how the traditional concepts of faith and reason might once again be brought into a closer relationship and included one of my guides in this journey, Derrida.

> Let us suppose that the inaugural and constituting act of modernity in the seventeenth century was an act of exclusion or bracketing: that the modern epoch turns on an *epoche*, a methodological imperative, in which modernity made up its mind to abide by human reason alone. In the *via moderna*, the rule will be that we are to make our way along a way...illuminated by the light of reason alone, of what was called reason in the seventeenth and eighteenth century. If that is so, then one way to think of the effect we were trying to provoke in this conference is to imagine its participants as engaged in the common pursuit of pushing past the constraints of this old, methodologically constricted, less enlightened, strait and narrow Enlightenment, which found it necessary to cast 'reason' and 'religion' in mortal opposition.
> (Derrida in Caputo and Scanlon (eds.) 1999, 2)

What this is hinting at is the possibility that both what is known as reason and what is normally included under the heading of faith or religion, can now be construed in other ways, and this might mean that other relationships between them become a possibility. This is not to claim that this will happen, but only that it might. One of the constant and inescapable problems of this discussion is that of exactly whose definitions or interpretations of these key terms one is using. After all, the objection of many Christians to the effects of the Kantian approach, was that the very meaning of the word faith was, from now on, determined by philosophers pursuing a separate agenda, rather than by people of faith themselves. There is no way around the questions of appropriation or of 'eating well'.

However, I do want to suggest that significant progress can be made if we follow this path and review the established meanings of both faith and reason. I will do this under the somewhat controversial heading of 'deconstruction' – a term that itself requires some explanation before we can go any further.

In many ways this term has become more of a hindrance than a help – just like the term 'postmodern' – simply because it is now used by a variety of people in quite different ways and often with potentially conflicting agendas. I will continue to use it, but with great caution, making it clear that I do not employ deconstruction as if it were some technique or tool of interpretation that could guarantee a movement of thought from A to B. This follows careful study of the ways in which Derrida himself – who first coined the term in its current context – employed this approach. Even to call it an approach is really to claim too much and Derrida himself fights shy of the suggestions that there is any one technique called 'deconstruction' that anybody else can simply pick up and then apply to a set of texts or ideas. What Derrida appears to be concerned to do is to identify the other possibilities, those which often lie hidden or unacknowledged, in certain texts in which he has taken an interest. Deconstruction – if there is such a thing – is a concern for the 'other', which is why it might be of interest in this discussion about faith as the 'other' of reason. I will offer a quotation from Derrida that I have found particularly helpful in this context and may lead us deeper into our debate.

> All that a deconstructive point of view tries to show, is that since convention, institutions and consensus are stabilizations…this means that they are stabilizations of something essentially unstable and chaotic. Thus, it becomes necessary to stabilize precisely because stability is not natural: it is because there is instability that stabilization becomes necessary: it is because there is chaos that there is a need for stability. Now, this chaos and instability, which is fundamental, founding and irreducible, is at once naturally the worst against which we struggle with laws, rules, conventions, politics and provisional hegemony, but at the same time it is a chance, a chance to change, to destabilize. If there were continual stability, there would be no need for politics, and it is to the extent that stability is not natural, essential or substantial, that politics exists and ethics is possible. Chaos is at once a risk, and a chance, and it is here that the possible and the impossible cross each other. (Derrida 1996, 84)

One meaning of this is that as soon as one defines a term or a concept, this represents an attempted stabilization of its meaning. This is what this word means so any other possible meanings are now excluded. Any careful study of our use of language reveals that such definitions, although not arbitrary, are invariably subject to destabilization and serve to suppress other possibilities which continue to lie dormant within the language. Poetry is the obvious example of a deliberate play upon the other possibilities of the meanings of words. One could argue that the same is true of notions of human identity. Once I define myself or present myself in a particular way – say as an upright and upstanding member of the community worthy of honour and respect – then certain aspects of human behaviour are supposedly ruled out as inconsistent with that identity. People like that do not do such things, and, if they do, they are deceiving themselves and us about their true identity. This tension creates problems for public figures such as politicians and ministers of religion let alone husbands and wives in settled and stable relationships. We all know however that every one of us is liable to fall from grace and betray such identities, thus supporting the view that they are indeed attempted stabilizations of an essential instability. Things could always be otherwise and sometimes are!

What Derrida is saying applies equally to all rules, laws and conventions. They are attempts to create stability and continuity, without which human society could not function, but which are always likely to slip out of control at a moment's notice. Some people are aware of this and learn to be comfortable with it whereas others seem intent on clinging onto the stabilizations for dear life, presumably afraid that to even acknowledge other possibilities would be to let the barbarians in through the gates and let loose the dogs of confusion and anarchy. Hence perhaps a deep resistance to the work of Derrida himself within certain circles. He is drawing to our attention certain aspects of human life that we would rather deny or ignore. It is always more comfortable to retain the veneer of stability and order or to stick to firm criteria of interpretation and definitions of identity.

These tensions between chaos and order, between instability and structure, go to the very heart of what I will present in this book. The intrusion of the 'other', the encounter with that which is different, the awareness of that within ourselves that does not conform to our external self-image, are all destabilizing factors and thus potential sources of fear. 'Deconstruction' – should there be such a thing – simply brings to the surface the other possibilities that are driven into hiding every time we settle for a stable interpretation or structure. It is not that we can avoid searching for stability and order because we are unable to survive in a state of permanent anarchy. Neither is it to argue that one of these approaches is correct in some way and that the other is unjustifiable. It is just to say that this is the way life is. We live within this tension between chaos and order and there are times – as Derrida says – when the chaos needs to break through because this is the only way in which things will ever change. One might argue that if faith in the form of Christianity is about transformation and change, then we ought to be able to welcome a degree of chaos and instability. Encountering the 'other' – whether that be a person or a set of ideas – is exactly the challenge that elicits a Christian response. However, this is to jump slightly ahead of ourselves.

For the moment I am arguing that 'deconstruction' – this giving of attention to the 'other' – is a possible means of reviewing the current stabilizations of the relationship between faith and reason and examining if other possibilities might be revealed.

Before I move on to the detail of this, a simple example from one of my practical involvements. My experience as a Board member of the Housing Association has brought me into contact, for the first time, with the world of corporate business plans. I was initially impressed with the way in which such plans attempted to project well into the future how the business might progress. Without such documents it is not possible to develop a strategy for working over coming months and years and identify tasks and objectives. Corporate business plans are massive attempts at stabilization. However, I soon became increasingly bemused by this process because it did not seem to portray a world that I could recognize. How could one know, with any degree of certainty, that interest rates or rates of inflation, for instance, would be at a certain level over such a period of time. One course, one cannot know such things, because life is essentially unpredictable and insecure. When you take the funerals of people who have had their lives planned out ahead of them assuming that nothing unforeseen can happen, you soon begin to encounter the chaos and disorder. These business plans did not seem to relate to the real world, yet, without them, no business can move into the future with any pattern or plan. Assumptions have to be made and a degree of order and continuity has to be projected into the future and I would argue that there is an element of faith involved in this. However, the business world claims to operate through rational design and decision making. Consultants get paid thousands of pounds to help us construct such designs. To admit the 'other' within the agreed façade of business life is almost unthinkable. It may be heresy to say this, but much of the business world appears to rest upon 'faith' – a confidence in a certain set of assumptions which can indeed be defended but might also turn out to be completely insecure – as well as upon the rationality that is its public face. In which case, perhaps there are other possibilities for the relationship between 'faith' and 'reason'!

Deconstructing reason

I am going to suggest that the prime candidate for a reformulated concept of reason that takes on board major contemporary criticisms is Habermas's communicative reason. I have dealt with the detail of this elsewhere (Reader 1997, Reader 2002) so do not intend to repeat that work here but do need to refer to some of Habermas's basic ideas in order to explain what follows.

The Enlightenment concept of human autonomy being founded upon our powers of reasoning became subject to a significant critique during the course of the twentieth century. The main thrust of this is that reason has become a strait-jacket or an 'iron cage', merely providing a set of techniques or processes that yield a truth in purely mechanical fashion. What it cannot do, simply because it claims to be neutral in terms of all sets of substantive values, is to provide any answers to questions of right and wrong. Hence reason as a way of thinking through the most efficient means of achieving certain aims can just as easily become the servant of evil human purposes as of good ones. If the objective is to exterminate a particular species or race, for instance, reason may enable one to identify the most effective way of doing this. It will not point out that such actions are morally unacceptable. It is this mechanical concept of reason – what is often called instrumental reason – that has become its dominant form through its application in science, technology and commerce and is now under the closest scrutiny as having led to a series of human crimes and tragedies (Bauman 1991).

However, thinkers such as Habermas have argued that this instrumental reason is only one of reason's possible forms. In fact, Habermas sees it as a distortion of what reason could and should achieve. The claim to neutrality has always been one of the concept's more controversial aspects and it has long been pointed out that there can be no such thing, since reason itself is part of a specific tradition that itself rests upon certain assumptions. These very assumptions cannot be argued into existence by using reason. One has to accept specific propositions as true before one can go on to argue the effectiveness of reason. What Habermas is saying is that this form of reason is part of a process of development that now needs to be challenged and then moved forward. His concept of communicative reason is just that. Rather than claiming that there is this neutral concept that is somehow plucked out of thin air without any further justification, he argues that the very nature and structure of language embodies certain assumptions that yield his concept of communicative reason. It is language as the most vital means of human communication that provides not the neutral, but still the universal ground for human reason. Reason cannot be reason – philosophically – unless it can claim to operate universally. It has to hold good in all contexts, regardless of cultural, religious or political differences. It has to be transcontextual. However, this claim is normally made at the expense of all other traditions of thought or human activity. So, for instance, all religious traditions would be deemed to be subject to its authority. Habermas believes that his concept of communicative reason does not determine the truth or otherwise of any other tradition; it does not impose upon Christianity an alien set of values or beliefs. If this were to be correct, then here might be an understanding of reason that was not automatically in conflict with notions of faith. Hence the potential significance of Habermas's ideas for our discussion.

It does also need to be said though that Habermas has a specific interpretation of the role of religion within human development. He holds a basically evolutionary view of human societies which attributes a place to religion within which those of faith might not themselves be comfortable. It is not that religion is now defunct in terms of its truth claims or social significance, which is often what sociologists and philosophers appear to claim when they utilize evolutionary notions. It is rather that religion, or those who continue to adhere to such traditions, must now be prepared to argue the case for their beliefs in the public arena and to offer support and justifications for where they stand and why. Gone are the days – according to Habermas – when one could just adhere to one's tradition in an unthinking or uncritical fashion. All traditions must be prepared to refine themselves through the fire of encounter with other traditions, accepting that their truth-claims need to be put to the test. If this is correct, then adherents must accept that their views and beliefs will be challenged and their subsequent position subject to change.

Now one can argue this on two grounds. One could hold, as Habermas does, that this is the consequence of a series of developments of human thought and social structure, that can both be identified empirically and justified intellectually.

This is the way that things were always going to happen once it became clear that different traditions were going to come into contact and conflict. That is a strong form of the argument. On the other hand, one could just say that this seems to be where things have got to and that this is the situation that people of faith are now facing, and this would be the view that I would adopt. I do believe that this idea that the Christian tradition – along with all others – now has to be prepared to be open, self-critical and reflexive about its beliefs and practices, reflects what I see happening around me. Whether or not one agrees with Habermas's more detailed arguments, it is possible to acknowledge that the tradition cannot claim immunity from critique and present itself as the only way to go without reference to other ideas and views. Now that we live in a pluralistic culture, let alone a globalized international society, it is impossible to avoid encounters with different and conflicting patterns of thought. To simply state that we have got it right and the rest have got it wrong, does not seem to me to be a recipe for peaceful progress, let alone for intellectual integrity. However, others may well disagree and I accept that there is a range of views within Christianity itself. This is my own stance on this, based very much on practical experience.

Having said all this it is necessary to offer a brief and critical examination of Habermas's ideas to see if one can identify the 'other' within his particular concept of reason. It needs to be remembered that this process does not intend to destroy nor to undermine the potential validity of his views, but to bring to the surface the other possibilities that remain hidden or unacknowledged.

Habermas presents four criteria for effective communication: understanding, truth, truthfulness or sincerity, and normative correctness. In other words, if human communication breaks down, here are a set of criteria by which one can judge what has gone wrong and what therefore needs to change. If one has misunderstood what another person is saying, or wants to test out whether or not one has understood correctly, one can stop the conversation and test this out. It is easy to ask 'Is this what you meant?' Similarly, one is often making judgements about whether or not the other person or persons are being sincere in what they are saying, or whether there is a deliberate intent to mislead. How often do we read the papers or listen to politicians on news broadcasts and say 'I do not believe this; they are trying to pull the wool over our eyes'? The criterion of normative correctness is simply a way of saying that it is either appropriate or inappropriate for certain people to make certain statements or take specific actions. So we might accept that it is in order to be flagged down for speeding on the motorway by a police patrol car, but not by a milk tanker. It is the remaining criterion, that of truth itself, that creates problems for Habermas. The other three can be seen to operate regardless of traditions or assumptions: they are just the way language is used across all cultures. But is it even possible to operate with a concept of truth that is neutral with regard to such traditions? Philosophers know that there are different concepts of truth and that these are open to debate and disagreement. A Christian might want to argue that truth is that which is revealed by God, say through Scripture or through experience as tested by the Christian community. Does Habermas himself then operate with a particular notion of truth rather than with a supposedly neutral concept?

Well, yes he does, once one begins to examine his work in greater depth. He operates with a view of truth as that which can be established through the process of rational argumentation. Even to say this begs the question of what one means by 'rational argumentation', but the detail of this is not essential for this discussion. The point is that he does not – and arguably cannot – operate without a particular concept of truth, one that belongs to a particular tradition and that would be contested by those outside it. How then can such a concept be transcontextual in the way that Habermas requires? Well, it cannot. But then, I would argue, neither could any other candidate for the notion of truth operate in a wholly neutral or transcontextual manner. It is one of those basic assumptions without which the whole system cannot operate. It is as fundamental to these criteria of effective communication as an assumption about future interest rates might be to a corporate business plan. Does this then invalidate Habermas's criteria completely and throw his concept of communicative reason on the scrap-heap? I do not believe that it does, particularly as his other criteria can more convincingly be argued to operate across cultural boundaries. What this does is to show that even such a clever reformulation of reason still continues to contain its 'other', a key point that cannot be decided according to its own criteria but which must be derived from elsewhere. But then, it could never be otherwise. No other system of reason could ever avoid starting from a specific assumption about the nature of truth. Once one is aware of Habermas's assumption one can agree with it or not, but one's own contrary assumption will play exactly the same role within the overall system. It is surely better to know and acknowledge one's starting point and then build it openly and reflexively into the subsequent debate than for it to remain hidden and unacknowledged.

Connected to Habermas's notion of truth is the very particular concept of the good with which he operates. What is good, for him, is that which comes about by the process of rational and autonomous co-operation. This has considerable repercussions for his ideas about deliberative democracy and a discourse ethics which both build upon the notion of communicative reason. Habermas believes that all those who are directly affected by any public decisions should have the opportunity to have their say before such decisions are made. This is clearly related to the tradition of liberal democracy espoused by many Western nations and not necessarily accepted by other political and religious systems. A Christian might or might not go along with this idea of full and effective participation. The vexed question of how to create political structures which can do justice to those individuals and circumstances which do not happen to fit the general rules is inescapable and will return when we come to examine Derrida's counter-point to Habermas's position shortly. However, many of us would probably argue that something like his interpretation of democracy is a good thing and should be adopted by Christians. The type of practical projects mentioned in the first chapter could be expected to work on the assumption that people should be directly involved in decisions affecting their lives and those of their communities. Certainly the pressure would be upon those who disagree to argue their case. Once again, though, here is an example of the 'other' of reason, that which derives from a very particular context and tradition, operating at the very heart of Habermas's system. How could it ever be otherwise?

The final area of his work where a similar pattern emerges is that of his view of what it is to be a human being. Closer examination of his writing brings to the surface a very particular interpretation of human nature, one that has much in common with what we would see as an Enlightenment view. Although Habermas does acknowledge the contribution of thinkers such as Freud and the idea that there is an unconscious dimension to each individual which has an impact upon our beliefs and behaviour, he still holds a essentially optimistic view of the human capacity to unearth and then deal with this level. In other words, the 'pathologies' or distortions in our communications that occur as a result of them, can be expected to be brought to the surface through counselling or other forms of self-analysis, and thereby rendered harmless or ineffective. Humans are then able to exercise a form of autonomy or conscious self-direction that is free from the influences of their own past. One achieves 'reflexivity', this ability to stand back and interpret one's views and behaviour and then decide to act otherwise, through the exercise of communicative reason at a personal or intimate level. It has to be said both that this is not the widely accepted interpretation of Freud's view of human nature and that it is challenged by other thinkers within the political field, notably many feminists. I would also not share such a sanguine view of what human beings can achieve in self-understanding through their own efforts, partly because of what I have learnt from these other thinkers and partly because it conflicts with my own experience of human nature as filtered through the Christian tradition. The details of this specific debate will be presented at a later stage as I believe it is probably the most significant area of insight into the subject of blurring boundaries. At this point however the object is simply to point out that Habermas does operate with a very particular notion of what it is to be a human being, one that might well not be shared by other contemporary thinkers. He holds a 'particular' in the midst of his transcontextual or 'universal' concept of reason.

Does this, in itself, invalidate the idea of communicative reason? I would argue not, because any other version of reason or any version of the 'other' traditions that might be in opposition to it, will also have to make assumptions about human nature. It is another of those key or grounding assumptions without which one cannot even get started on the important debates. Awareness of one's beliefs and assumptions is at least a means of raising the significance of such ideas for all further discussions. One is bound to be taking a stand on notions of truth, of value and of human nature, whenever one engages in significant debate about what one should be doing and why. If Habermas is correct that we now need to open our traditions to critical examination then this awareness of one's own starting points is surely essential to the process. This does not mean the end of discussion and a retreat to entrenched positions, but rather a 'laying of one's cards on the table' in order to see what progress can then be made. This is where the other aspects of Habermas's concept of communicative reason can then come into play. It will be more honest to admit the influence of the 'other' within both reason and faith from the outset of such discussions.

The impossibility of faith

Having examined the possibilities of a relationship between reason and faith from the side of the former and realized that reason itself has to work upon certain assumptions that cannot be justified internally, we now need to view the same area from the side of faith. Is any form of relationship between the two either possible or desirable? In order to do this I will refer briefly to some work of Derrida who appears to provide the most effective counter-point to Habermas's rationalistic approach.

Although Derrida is a philosopher and may not immediately be identified with an interest in matters of faith (Caputo 1997), he has latterly written on the theme of religion and its relationship with reason (Derrida and Vattimo 1998). It is however a slightly earlier book that offers us the best clues as to the problems that religion will have with a philosophical and indeed ethical stance (Derrida 1995). In this text he examines in detail the story of Abraham and Isaac and the former's willingness to sacrifice his son in order to obey God's command. Derrida is perhaps less interested in the original version from Genesis than he is in the interpretation of the story offered by Kierkegaard in his *Fear and Trembling*.

One of the prominent suggestions that Kierkegaard makes is that God is so wholly other, so totally beyond the realm of human articulation and understanding, that he does not have to share with human beings his reasons for anything that he does, or for any command that he gives to those who believe in him. In fact, were he to give his reasons he would not be God, because then he would be operating at the same level as his creatures and this is what is not possible. So there is a secret, or an impossibility, involved when God commands Abraham to sacrifice his son. No reasons can be given for this command. Abraham himself is then caught up in the same dynamic. He also cannot give any justification for what he is about to do. He is bound to keep the secret, partly because he also does not have access to an explanation. However, according to Kierkegaard's understanding of what we call ethics, this refusal to speak about this potential action transgresses the ethical domain. There is a conflict between his obedience to God and the singularity of that relationship and situation and the normal human demand to articulate one's reasons for a specific action in the light of more general structures of behaviour.

What is being suggested here is that it is the movement into language, the requirement to express ourselves in terms to which other humans can relate, that betrays our relationship with God as wholly other and indeed deprives us of our singularity or our uniqueness as individual human beings. Hence any form of philosophy or any version of morality, both of which are essentially public in nature and require the use of language, are in direct contradiction with the religious life. All articulation is a betrayal of faith and the only possible appropriate response to the call of God is silence. This then is to describe the difference between reason and faith in the most extreme manner. On this understanding there can be no relationship whatsoever. Even to obey God 'out of duty' is to contravene this directive since the very concept of duty links human actions to a wider and thus articulated structure of beliefs. To put it at its crudest, Abraham's action in obeying God is a 'one off', it cannot be explained or justified in relation to any framework of action or belief. But then, according to Kierkegaard – or to Derrida's interpretation of him – all genuine Christianity is like this. The notion of singularity, that which is unique, unrepeatable and beyond articulation, is central to an appropriate understanding of faith.

One might object that this is so extreme a view as to bear no obvious relationship to normal life. Yet Derrida points out that this is not the case. On any occasion when one responds to another human being, one is being called upon to make a form of sacrifice. By responding to one particular person in need one is having to sacrifice the possibility of responding to somebody else who is in need, simply because it is not possible to give one's attention to everybody who deserves it. Such a decision is both inescapable and impossible to justify. Imagine receiving begging letters through the post from a variety of different charities. Unless one has unlimited resources and an unlimited capacity for sympathy and identification with others, one will decide to respond to one or two and ignore the rest. When making that decision it is clear that most of the requests, if not all, were probably equally valid calls upon one's attention and money. However, one cannot do everything. This requires a sacrifice, a willingness to choose 'x' instead of 'y' knowing that 'y' had an equally justified call upon one's response. Every time one puts one's own family or friends at the top of a list of priorities, one is doing the same thing.

> ...what binds me thus in my singularity to the absolute singularity of the other, imme-
> diately propels me into the space of risk or absolute sacrifice. There are also others, an
> infinite number of them, the innumerable generality of others to whom I should be

33

bound by the same responsibility, a general and universal responsibility (what Kierkegaard calls the ethical order). I cannot respond to the call, the request, the obligation,
or even the love of another without sacrificing the other other, the other others.

(Derrida 1995, 68)

If this is the case, and one can see the force of Derrida's argument here, then
even philosophy or reason in the form of ethics, is impossibly different from the
demands of faith. The two are simply entirely different and alien orders of activity.
Responding to the couple who turn up on my doorstep needing accommodation,
or even to the person involved in the accident on the motorway are both singularities, not examples of a more general or universal directive to behave in a particular
way. Yet reason requires a structure that is transcontextual if not universal, a means
of describing and justifying one's action in relation to other criteria or patterns of
belief. The 'other' which is faith is thus so wholly other as to defy articulation yet
alone justification.

Derrida, however, having established this most extreme interpretation, then
proceeds to present an alternative. He is acutely aware that the idea that one can
witness to such a faith commitment in absolute silence – which is what this view
would entail – is itself impossible. How would it ever be possible to communicate
to others the content of faith without moving into the realm of language? Of course
it is not possible to avoid articulating one's faith, however singular or unique the
experience behind it. One could also argue that, once one moves into the domain of
language, one enters the sphere of communicative reason as described by Habermas.
Even Abraham, sooner or later, had he actually gone through with the sacrifice of
his son, would have had to explain to somebody what he had done and why. How
would he have explained this one to his wife, for instance? Some form of witness or
testimony will be called for, despite the singularity of God's demand and Abraham's
response. Hence the 'other' which is reason will impinge upon the singularity that is
faith. This may mean compromise, even a betrayal, that which cannot be explained
falling into the traps of language with its many possible meanings and different
levels, but is there really any alternative? Some relationship between faith and reason
is required even though one can never do justice to the 'other' through language.

Perhaps the finest description of this dilemma, this impossibility that nevertheless
has to be faced, is that given by the philosopher Levinas – both influenced by and
an influence upon Derrida. He talks of this as the difficulty of relating the Saying
to the Said (Levinas 1981). The Saying is the direct point of contact with the other
person, what he calls my exposure to the other, the face-to-face encounter that calls
forth my response. This indeed can never be reduced to mere words. I either respond
in that moment of encounter or refuse to respond. The Said is then the ways in
which one articulates, turns into language and explanations, the purposes behind
one's action. Such statements are then subject to rational debate and testing. They

will fail to do justice to what one has done, or not done, but they are an inescapable dimension of the responsibility we have to the third person – the other 'other' who was not directly involved. Giving an account of one's actions both to oneself, but especially to others who are significant in one's life, is simply what is required by virtue of human relationship let alone social mores. Thus the Saying is reduced to the Said in the knowledge that what is then said will never fully capture the depth of the original encounter. There will always be a residue of what is unsaid within the Said, that which points to the Saying but only inadequately. Releasing the 'other' within what is articulated is a matter of opening up this residue of the unsaid said within the reduced Said. There will be a constant back and forward movement between these two possibilities as one struggles to put into language the depth of encounter with the other person.

What all of this points us toward is the need for faith to find a relationship to what we call reason. The singularity of the religious experience, whether that is a moment of revelation or an encounter with another person, requires, sooner or later, an engagement with the compromised world of human communication. One cannot finally witness in silence – or perhaps one should say that this is the extreme limit of faith and may be the only way on certain occasions. The articulation of the encounter could be described as a 'mediated singularity', always accepting that the mediation participates in the betrayal that is language – the attempt to place the unique individual or experience into a general or universal category. As we have noted earlier, this will always result in something being lost or remaining unacknowledged. Deconstruction – should it exist – is the intention to bring to the surface what which is 'other', that which has been forced underground once language takes over. This process can never be completed, but remains as an obligation and responsibility. What I intend to show next is that there are ways of relating faith and reason that may help us to evaluate those practical experiences of blurred encounters. When is it possible to say that faith is 'eating well' in its encounter with contemporary culture?

3

Locating the Other

Unconditional hospitality

One day during the summer of 2003 my elder son had his moment of fame. He appeared briefly on a national news item which highlighted the problem of gang-masters using and exploiting migrant workers for poorly-paid fruit picking. My son's then boss was interviewed as an employer within the business who made sure that he only employed workers who were paid and treated properly. Apparently, these gangmasters collect migrant workers from picking-up points in Birmingham and then drive them out to Worcestershire to work long hours for inadequate rewards. This issue had been brought to national attention because there had recently been a bad accident on a level crossing just outside Evesham in which a minibus carrying such workers had been struck by a London-bound train, carrying, amongst others, the Bishop of Hereford and a local MP. A number of workers in the minibus were killed and the driver appeared to have fled the scene. There was a suggestion that the driver did not know or understand how to use these farm-based level crossings which required that he stop the vehicle and phone through to see whether or not a train was on its way. Having failed to do this the van was then struck. Could this particular driver even speak English? As one might imagine, this became, albeit briefly, a matter of local controversy. It raised the wider question of how we treat those people who come across to this country each year for the fruit-picking season, quite often from Eastern Europe, in order to earn more than they could back home. The previous year there had been a fatal stabbing amongst such a group where it was believed that a national rivalry or argument had led to violence. There seems to be a sort of shadow world of such workers. This is of benefit to employers who need access to willing – and possibly cheap – labour, and to the workers themselves who can earn better rates provided they are prepared to put up with the terms and conditions. However, even in the middle of apparently tranquil and civilized Worcestershire, the issue of how to locate the 'other' is clearly a live one!

Strangely, perhaps, a site within a short distance of where this accident took place had also recently been designated by the government as one of the locations for its centres for asylum seekers. One needs to remember that this is open countryside with the city of Worcester some twelve miles away as the nearest centre of population. The surrounding area is one of scattered villages and hamlets and two small market towns. Communications in the form of public transport are limited to say the least, and there are very few sources of entertainment or easily accessible social life. The site was one where, just the year before, sheep carcasses from the Foot and Mouth outbreak of 2001 had been buried. Not surprisingly there had been much local opposition to this proposal. Even the two bishops in the diocese found themselves opposing this suggestion backed by local churches on the grounds that this was simply an unsuitable and inadequate site without the appropriate facilities. There was also the wider question of whether this way of handling the problem of asylum seekers was acceptable in the first place. The bishops were perhaps a little embarrassed to find themselves backing the same case as local people whose arguments could have been characterized as 'NIMBY-ism', even though the grounds of their objections were different. Either way, it felt as though there was not going to be a welcome in the 'white highlands' of Worcestershire for this particular group of people. Contrast that then with the obvious willingness to accept foreigners into the home country when it was a matter of commercial advantage or 'good business'!

It is easy to be judgemental about such matters from the outside. The issues behind both cases are complex and there is right and wrong on both sides. What this highlights though are the real difficulties involved in encountering and locating the other, particularly when there are serious cultural and economic differences at stake. Worcestershire is hardly alone in facing these and certainly fares neither better nor worse than other parts of the UK in handling these difficulties. What are the appropriate limits to hospitality? When is it justified to close the door in the face of the stranger and tell him to go away? In crossing the boundaries between faith and reason – for instance – when does faith need to pull up the drawbridge in order to protect itself from an alien invasion?

I wish to refer once again to some theoretical resources from the work of Derrida which I believe illuminate the difficulties of an unconditional hospitality. He acknowledges that the task of setting limits to who enters one's territory is an inescapable one and that there have to be criteria, or sets of rules, which govern who is acceptable and who is not. However, once we do this we also have to realize that we are then setting limits to hospitality itself and this may appear to contravene both religious ideals of welcoming the other, and also the ideals behind the human rights discourse that could be argued to be the secular version of those religious ideals.

> We have to be aware that, to the extent that we are looking for criteria, for conditions, for passports, borders and so on, we are limiting hospitality, hospitality as such, if there is such a thing. I'm not sure there is pure hospitality. But if we want to understand what hospitality means, we have to think of unconditional hospitality, that is, openness to whomever, to any newcomer. And of course, if I want to know in advance who is the

good one, who is the bad one – in advance! – if I want to have an available criterion to distinguish between the good immigrant and the bad immigrant, then I would have no relation to the other as such. So to welcome the other as such, you have to suspend the use of criteria.   (Derrida in Caputo and Scanlon 1999, 133)

Derrida is clear that he is not recommending that one suspends the search for criteria, particularly in the realms of practical politics, but he is saying that unless we have a grasp of what unconditional hospitality might be, then we have no way of judging our practical responses to the 'other'. We need to see how far our criteria themselves measure up to the ideal of an unconditional hospitality, because without this we have no real sense of our relationship with those who might need our help. What becomes evident from this – and this is invariably the fear that drives governments and people to support hard-line approaches to the issue – is that there are risks involved in welcoming the other across the boundaries. Whether it is the individual householder allowing the stranger across the threshold and into the house, even though he might be a threat to one's own family, or the state allowing asylum seekers across the national border even though they might be terrorists planning some atrocity, the issue is the same. When and how do we judge that the risks are too great and close down entry? How do we then stand with the directive to respond to others who are in need? As Derrida suggests, there are no satisfactory answers to this dilemma, but neither can we cease to keep struggling with it.

As is also fairly obvious, it is the refugee or the asylum seeker who is the most clear-cut challenge to our supposedly liberal attitude to the blurring or crossing of boundaries. Although there are always other 'others' internally who pose questions and threats to our security, at least they will have some official status within our borders and can be dealt with accordingly if they transgress. This status is also their protection against misunderstanding and prejudice – in theory. However, those who slip through the net, for whatever reasons, do not have such a clear status and may fear for themselves should something go wrong. I am thinking about the driver of the minibus who fled the scene of the crash. He should probably not have been driving the vehicle in the first place, but did he have a choice in the matter? Where would he stand within our legal system if this was the case? Every state must have ways of policing its frontiers and establishing criteria for entry. One can widen the range of the borders and alter the criteria as the European Union is trying to do, but there still have to be borders and restrictions somewhere if the Union is to have any meaning. Hence there will always be those who are outside the boundaries.

Later in the chapter I will take the subject of human rights as itself a boundary issue for faith in order to develop criteria for judging the possible relationship between reason and faith. Human rights could be seen as one way in which reason comes to terms with the question of locating the other, often within a legal or political framework. How does it measure up by the criterion of unconditional hospitality? However, it also has a boundary with faith responses to the matter of offering a welcome to the other and it is this that will be of interest to us. I now offer this quote from a key text on human rights to support the suggestion that it is the refugee who creates the greatest challenge to both codes of practice. Who is the 'other' who demands my response according to human rights? Who is my neighbour according to the teaching of Jesus? When and how does either tradition set limits and decide to locate the other beyond the boundary?

> Lack of community and total absence of rights turn the refugee into the absolute, total threatening other. Beyond the embrace of family and group, and outside the protection of the law, the refugee is reduced to the status of naked, abstract humanity, an exemplum of universal human nature before it becomes concrete through the individualizing action of community and equalizing effect of the law. The refugee is so radically different from us that no similarity can be found or equivalence constructed. She is the symbol of difference as such, she represents nothing but her own absolutely unique individuality, which deprived of all recognition or protection is as deadly as death is totally singular. (Douzanis 2000, 365)

If there are echoes in this of the ideas with which we closed the previous chapter, of the singularity of Abraham in his obedience to God's command, then this should not surprise us. How do the human structures of either law or religion deal with the unique individual who claims to be acting outside or beyond conventional boundaries? It is precisely the singularity which presents the greatest challenge to all frameworks constructed through human language. Yet without the singularity how could there ever have been the insight or revelation behind either faith or reason? In essence, the question of locating the other or of setting boundaries for self-protection is another manifestation of Levinas's tension between the Saying and the Said.

Locating the relationship between faith and reason

Having established in chapter two that some relationship between reason and faith is at least a possibility, the task now is to identify locations where this relationship might be pursued. It is crucial to be aware of the limits of this enterprise. It is not an attempt to say that faith and reason are actually the same, nor that they are the same in these particular respects. It is pointing towards areas of common interest where conversations between the two might fruitfully be pursued. The conversations themselves must not be pre-empted nor pre-judged. It may be that the only conclusion possible is that there is nothing more to be said and that the discussion will cease. It may be that one or both parties will decide that there is a case for closing the boundaries between the two and staying safely behind locked doors for fear of invasion. The risk of 'contamination' may be just too great. However, even a failed attempt at communication may prove illuminating in the long run, so it is with that proviso that I offer the following.

I believe that it is possible to identify four locations where the relationship between faith and reason might constructively be pursued. Having described those I will then go on to show how these areas are of potential value in the practical domain of the current debate between Christianity and the human rights tradition. Perhaps it would be too strong to argue that the locations provide criteria for deciding whether or not it is possible or desirable to cross the boundary between the two traditions, but, as we have just seen, this could indeed be a valid objective for the enterprise. If these criteria to be developed are met in this particular instance, then there may well be a case for establishing and continuing a relationship between Christianity and the discourse of human rights. That judgement must await further exploration.

The four locations are to be found from within the contrasting work of Habermas and Derrida already identified as being of interest. In summary they are: a concern with the messianic as a structure of human experience; the tension between the universal and the particular (the Saying and the Said); a shared interest in the nature of human subjectivity and finally the realization that there is a tension between determinacy and indeterminacy as soon as one enters the realm of practical politics.

The Messianic

We have already caught glimpses of the utopian elements in Habermas's reconstructed concept of reason. It needs to be remembered that Habermas was once of a more explicitly Marxist persuasion, searching for a version of Critical Theory that would provide a purchase upon contemporary culture and reveal the grounds for a better society. Despite his later appropriation of ideas from other sources there continues to be a future-orientated aspect to his theories. Even though his four criteria for effective communication appear to be grounded in current language use, it is undoubtedly the case that they cannot operate without a vision of a different and better future. He works on the assumption that it is possible to clear up misunderstandings between people and to make the meaning of sentences accessible and transparent. He also assumes that it is possible to achieve levels of trust between people and to judge their sincerity – or lack of it – within what they say to one another. Even when it comes to the key area of truth Habermas has to assume that it is possible to establish agreed understandings and concepts from which to operate. One could argue that each of these require an optimistic view of human nature simply because much human communication displays exactly the opposite of what Habermas is seeking. However – and here there is a direct parallel with the notion of unconditional hospitality – unless there were such optimistic and visionary hopes for the future, how could one have criteria against which to evaluate current practice? So it is not that this is how things are most of the time, but how things might and even should be, and unless we have some vision of this there is no way of judging where we are now. The concept of communicative reason shares with that of unconditional hospitality what Derrida might call a messianic structure.

If we turn then to Derrida, a superficial reading of his work might suggest that he stands at exactly the opposite pole to Habermas on the subject of human communication. After all his work on deconstruction would seem to emphasize destabilization and discontinuity, all the factors which work against establishing clear and objective meaning. It is the 'other' which remains hidden that is always likely to come to the surface and disrupt interpretations and communication. However, this built-in uncertainty in language itself only makes sense if one assumes that meaning and understanding are at least horizons for human communication. For Derrida they may be somewhat more distant than they are for Habermas, but they are there nevertheless. There is, to use Derrida's terminology, a messianic expectation that agreement may be achieved and must be the ultimate objective.

Derrida's ideas on the messianic are worthy of much deeper exploration but can only be touched upon here (see Caputo 1997, James H. Olthius [ed.] 2002). He is concerned to show that there is a structure of human behaviour focused upon the future which can be identified in a number of different areas, not all of them explicitly religious. This despite the fact that the idea of a Messiah derives from the religions of the book, Judaism, Islam and Christianity. Thus the same structure is to be found within the concepts of both justice and democracy: both are always 'still to come'. It is when people start claiming that they have arrived, that they have taken definitive and final shape in the form of a particular historical configuration, that the trouble really begins. To carry out aggressive acts on the basis that this is to defend or to construct democracy is likely to be open to question. Thus for instance the invasion of Iraq in 2003 on the grounds that it would uncover weapons of mass destruction is a contemporary example of this. Whose version of democracy are we talking about here and exactly how close to the ideal of democracy are those who are claiming it as their own? The same questions must always apply to the notion of justice. Both place before us a horizon which remains ahead and unattainable, but one which allows us to judge how far we still have to travel. Once again there is an obvious parallel with the notion of unconditional hospitality mentioned in the previous section. As with the vision of the Messiah, he is always still to arrive and, if we believed that he had arrived and that we could now 'pin him down' in some way, we would be bound to be mistaken. It is those who claim to have identified and then appropriated the Messiah who then become a danger to the rest of us!

It seems to me therefore that one can see that both Habermas as the representative of reason and Derrida as a potential advocate of faith hold a concept of hope, an expectation for the future which both provide means of evaluating the present and some common ground for future exploration. This is not to say that they hold the same vision of the future, although both do place an emphasis upon language and human communication, but that they both perceive a structure or a horizon that could be a location for further discussion. Some understanding of the notion of the messianic appears to be a basic assumption that might well be found in the domains of both reason and faith and it is where this is to be found that there might be a fruitful crossing of the boundary between the two.

The Universal and the Particular

This is by now familiar territory and takes us straight back to the previous chapter's discussion on the impossibility of faith. It has always been part of the brief of reason to try to claim that it is of universal significance. We have seen that Habermas places his trust in the procedures of communicative reason in order to provide the transcontextual or universal elements of reason rather than depending upon any specific content. For reason, Christianity is a scandal simply because it rests upon a particular set of events derived from a specific period in history and thus unable to claim for itself the necessary universality. However, if reason is a matter of procedure rather than content, this should not matter – according to Habermas. Yet we have already had cause to question whether Habermas can convincingly evacuate his concept of communicative reason of all specific content and merely rely upon procedure as he claims. After all, he too relies upon a very particular notion of truth and indeed an understanding of the good as that which is established through rational autonomous co-operation. In which case, even his concept of reason rests upon certain specific and particular elements or assumptions. I have suggested that it is impossible to do otherwise and that this does not, of itself, invalidate his reconfiguration of reason. It might be suggested also that every universal of this sort has to contain a particular. There is no way in which one can enter this discussion without making some assumptions that cannot themselves be justified from within the system. Hence, from the side of philosophy, it may be impossible to separate the universal from the particular in the purist fashion that is often demanded. The two live in constant tension, pulling in different directions, but always finally in need of each other. Thus the relationship has to be carried on in this uneasy way.

From the other side of the relationship, that of the particularity of faith, there is also the inescapable tension of having to be able to articulate the content of one's beliefs or insights using the inadequate tools of language. As we gleaned from the story of Abraham and Isaac, is it finally possible to witness in silence, when explanations and justifications of one's actions will be required by others? The singularity of the personal religious experience would otherwise have to remain private and inaccessible to others and it is hard then to see how religious tradi-tions could even be formed. Yet as soon as one enters the realm of language one is crossing the boundary into the universal dimensions of human communication.

Every particular, in order to gain articulation, must allow itself to be compromised with that which is transcontextual or universal. To establish religious traditions, singularities must be turned into 'mediated singularities' through the medium of language or other forms of communication. Once again then I would argue that the 'pure' boundary between universal and particular cannot be held intact and that a degree of 'transgressing' is essential and inevitable. We shall see shortly that this is also true for other sets of ideals, not simply those of Christianity, in which case this is another area or location which may prove fruitful for a continuing relationship between faith and reason.

Human subjectivity

Habermas, despite trying to do justice to other levels of human subjectivity, notably that of the unconscious, still adheres to what seems to be a familiar Enlightenment notion of the human subject. His optimism on the possibility of pathologies or distortions in communication being ironed out through counselling or psychoanalysis points to his belief that humans are indeed capable of understanding themselves once they have given the unconscious sufficient time and attention. Thus the rational dimension of our being is given precedence over concerns for the domain of feelings, needs and desires. Habermas also risks misrepresenting Freud's own understanding of the unconscious as always containing elements which resist interpretation and articulation. There are parts of ourselves of which we are never going to be fully aware and which continue to affect our behaviour in ways that we ourselves will not be able to alter. Hence there would be limits to the sort of reflexivity that is required by Habermas. The question here is not that of being true to anybody's particular theory, but of working out which view of human subjectivity most closely matches our experience. As with his views on language and on the possibility of achieving a universal that eschews all particulars, I would argue that Habermas is being unrealistically optimistic and that maybe Freud – if that is a correct interpretation of him – had a point.

Once again it is Derrida who offers an immediate counter-point to Habermas's view. He does this not in order to undermine reason or to suggest that it does not have a role to play, but rather to point out its limitations. I will return to this whole area in greater detail later in the book because I believe it is capable of further development in relation to our wider issue, but some mention of his views is clearly necessary at this stage. Derrida suggests that there is always a pre-autonomous encounter with the other, a moment which precedes conscious choice or response, and without which it makes no sense to talk of either autonomy or heteronomy. This idea has much in common with Levinas's idea of the primacy of the face-to-face encounter which he argues is the very basis of what we call ethics. Thus both Derrida and Levinas use such terms as 'welcome', 'hospitality', 'hostage' and 'proximity' to try to point us towards a level of human response that our familiar language of autonomy cannot describe. In a sense we are right back to the initial reaction of opening the front door and being confronted by somebody unknown. That very first response which, by its very nature, has to be spontaneous and almost instinctive, is the real basis for any further relationship. You either 'get it wrong' in that unguarded moment, or you create the potential trust that can lead to help and support. There is simply no time to stand back and work out how to respond to this person according to a predetermined set of criteria. I respond to this other person as if they were indeed 'my neighbour' or I do not and there may be no second chance to adjust one's reaction. Derrida also uses the phrase 'acquiescing to the testimony of the other' to describe what is required if trust is to be established (Derrida 1999). He does not restrict this to the use of language, although it can clearly also be applied to the acceptance of certain assumptions taken on trust from others. This is something that we do all the time, not just in our personal lives, but also in the 'rational' areas of business and science. Unless we were prepared to accept some views or interpretations on trust, even in those domains, we could never begin our discussions, even if we subsequently challenge those views.

At this point I do not want to question this perspective on human subjectivity in any more detail because although I do believe that it tells us something of significance about human nature that Habermas and other Enlightenment-based views are at risk of ignoring, I also believe that it is only part of a fuller picture that has yet to emerge. Neither the pre-autonomous nor the autonomous levels as described by Derrida, Levinas and Habermas offer the whole story. However, I hope that it is now clear that this area of human subjectivity is a potentially rich and fruitful location in which to pursue the relationship between reason and faith.

Democracy and indeterminacy

Habermas is well known as being an advocate of democracy and has indeed contributed work on what he and others call deliberative democracy (Bohman and Rehg [eds.] 1997). His idea is that all those who are potentially affected by a decision should have a voice in the process whereby that decision is made. He also incorporates this idea into his work on developing a discourse ethics (Habermas 1992). As with other aspects of his work it is clear that he holds an optimistic view of what can be achieved through the methods he supports. Rational autonomous cooperation is presupposed as a working principle throughout his writing on political matters with the hope of reaching consensus a major objective. However, whether such an objective is either possible or desirable is seriously open to question. For instance, it could be argued that consensus would really mean the suppression of minority views and this could include those of faith communities. One only needs to think of the disagreements surrounding abortion to understand how this could be so.

Those from a religious background might also feel that truth, or perhaps correct action, cannot be decided on the basis of democracy, however inclusive. If they hold to a strong doctrine of revelation then they would not agree to see this overruled by any sort of democratic process. It would still feel like an alien principle derived from the Enlightenment tradition and resting on a particular understanding of reason determining how and where the views of faith traditions should fit into the wider political process. One might also want to question Habermas's deeply held hope that deliberative democracy can, in any case, so readily yield the right or acceptable decision.

It is here that Derrida once again provides a crucial counter-point. As we might imagine, in his eyes democracy is still to come: it is another messianic concept pointing towards a future that we might not even recognize were it ever to be encountered. Yet it is necessary as an ideal against which to judge current practice. However, it is his analysis of the decision-making processes that creates deeper doubts about Habermas's optimism. Derrida is clear that each time we make a real decision, and by that he means a decision where we know that we could equally well have decided otherwise, then there is an element of uncertainty and indeterminacy about the process. In other words, if the 'decision' is clear-cut and it is obvious that there is only one course of action to be followed, then this is not really a decision at all. The 'decision' makes itself almost and we have no true choices to make. Of course we know that most significant decisions – those over which we struggle and agonize – are not like that. The problems come precisely when it is not clear which is the correct path to follow. In many of these cases it could well be that another decision could have been equally valid and that following another path will always leave that doubt in our minds. As with the example of choosing to offer help to one person at the expense of another, the decision itself appears somewhat arbitrary and it is difficult to articulate let alone justify why we took this decision and not another.

The danger of this approach is that it may paralyse us into a state of indecision. What are we supposed to do when either or a number of decisions appear equally possible? Politicians of course are paid and expected to make exactly those sorts of decisions and are invariably criticized whichever decision they make. There comes a point where a decision must be made and one just has to get on with it. Rationalizations may well be offered in retrospect, but the element of indeterminacy and uncertainty remains. No democratic process, however inclusive, can avoid the nature of such decisions. Hence Habermas's expectations of deliberative democracy seem too optimistic and need to be seen in the light of what could be called human finitude. Yet this is not to abandon democracy nor to suggest replacing it by another principle of political order. Derrida himself advocates democracy, but as an ideal to be striven for not an objective that can be claimed to have been obtained. It seems to me that the task of retaining the tension between these two approaches is a valid and important one and offers faith traditions a way of relating to the best of contemporary political ideals and processes. One can both support a version of democracy such as Habermas's whilst holding on to a critical perspective on it in the light of its inherent indeterminacy and uncertainty. So here is another location where there might be creative and fruitful interaction between faith and reason.

Christianity and human rights: testing the locations

Having established the four locations I now want to evaluate them by applying them to a particular example. As hinted at earlier I believe that the developing discourse on human rights is of significance for a faith-based relationship with contemporary culture. A major reason for this is that human rights are often offered as the contemporary secular means of judging and creating appropriate responses to others who are in need. The extent to which this developing tradition itself derives ideas and motivations from the Christian tradition is an interesting question, but it seems to me that we have now moved beyond this to a point where the two are more likely to be seen in opposition, or where the one has superseded the other.

Two recent practical examples must suffice. First there is the growing controversy over a possible constitution for the European Union. There are those within the Union who want to expunge any reference to a religious or Christian heritage for this new body of states. Whether such an approach is explicitly anti-Christian or simply wants no reference to any religion on the basis that this is now a secular constitution is not always clear. It often feels anti-Christian and therefore damaging to any potential relationship between church and state, but it may simply be the next stage of the Enlightenment view that matters of faith should be kept entirely separate from politics and public life. This is another version of the universal versus the particular argument. France is certainly at pains to keep other religious observances at bay and there has been a controversy towards the end of 2003 over their government banning Muslim headscarves in schools. This seems like an extreme version of the reason against faith debate, but it does show how prevalent and influential it is even if other countries do not want to go quite that far. Some Christian leaders are understandably concerned by and critical of this movement within the European constitution. It can be seen both as a battle for the heart of Europe and as a deeper conflict over the role of religion in public life. In a sense it is perhaps the prime example of the faith-reason dichotomy that I am concerned about in this book. If the secularists in this particular conflict win the day it will leave faith traditions in an increasingly isolated position in terms of political life and, I would argue, far more likely to engage in extremist action in order to gain a hearing. However, if they are included in the processes, on whose terms will they be allowed in on the debates and exactly what sort of influence will they be able to bring to bear? Who will be appropriating whom and who will be 'eating well'? Those of us who have caught glimpses of faith traditions being included at a lower level of decision-making processes are aware of the ambiguities and complexities of this type of involvement, particularly over the issue of representation. This is one of the problems of faith communities being drawn into democratic structures, but then, the alternative may be even less palatable.

The other current example is that of the detention of terrorist suspects without trial following the events of 9/11. The Archbishop of Canterbury argued in an article in the *Sunday Times* at the end of 2003 that this could well damage relationships with the Muslim community, something that he has been working hard to foster since those events. Amnesty International along with a government sub-committee has been arguing along similar lines but very much on human rights grounds. The human rights agenda would be expected to count against such action, the only possible exception being where the state believes its security is at stake and such detentions therefore justified. Without going into the details of this one can see that this is a classic example of Derrida's point about hospitality. How does one treat the stranger, the 'other', when one is in fear that this person might be about to do violence to one's own people or to otherwise undermine the political order? There have to be boundaries, restrictions and forms of self-protection, but then they are bound to act against the ethical directive to respond to the other person who is in need, or to contravene their human rights in these extreme circumstances. There may also be questions of the ways in which governments are using peoples' fears to manipulate circumstances to their own advantage. However, that is politics! And there is the problem once again. How does one realistically apply faith principles to the political order which operates along different lines? As we shall now see, the human rights tradition has exactly the same problems and appears to have at least some common ground with communities of faith. We can now see though that these are real and significant practical questions needing to be addressed.

1. Human rights and the messianic

One does not need to look very deeply into the human rights literature to realize that there is a powerful messianic component at work. Although it is clear that they are, on one level, to do with regulating the here and now, they are as much about the future and providing criteria by which to judge the present as simply about regulation. For instance, the European Union has been drafting a Charter of Fundamental Rights, and part of the preamble to this makes it clear that this is as much a statement of good intentions as a description of current reality.

> Conscious of its spiritual and moral heritage, the Union is founded on the indivisible, universal values of human dignity, freedom, equality and solidarity; it is based on the principles of democracy and the rule of law. It places the individual at the heart of

its activities, by establishing the citizenship of the Union and by creating an area of freedom, security and justice. The Union contributes to the preservation and to the development of these common values while respecting the diversity of the cultures and traditions of the peoples of Europe as well as the national identities of the Member states and the organization of their public authorities at national, regional and local level…   (Draft Charter as of 28 September 2000)

On reading this one immediately begins to ask some serious questions. Using such terms as democracy, solidarity and justice suggests that these states of affairs already exist. However, we all know that this is far from being the case. So what is the point of such language? It is surely more a statement of intent, a set of ideals for the future, than a reflection of positions now achieved. Hence the messianic component. This is equally true though of all similar documents which build upon the human rights traditions. It is all too easy to point out that the twentieth century, despite being apparently the era of human rights, has seen the largest scale and most blatant contraventions of those rights in human history. As Douzanis says:

> If the twentieth century is the epoch of human rights, their triumph is, to say the least, something of a paradox. Our age has witnessed more violations of their principles than any of the previous and less 'enlightened' epochs. The twentieth century is the century of massacre, genocide, ethnic cleansing, the age of the Holocaust. At no point has there been a greater gap between the poor and the rich in the Western world and between the north and the south globally… No wonder then why the grandiose statements of concern by governments and international organizations are often treated with popular derision and skepticism.   (Douzanis 2000, 2)

The gap between the aspirations and the reality is distressingly wide and one wonders whether the grand statements serve any purpose whatsoever. Even worse, when they are used by governments and politicians one might question whether they are simply a blind for their exact opposite. So we return to the problems of such language as highlighted by Derrida. As soon as claims are made to have achieved or to have moved significantly towards these goals one needs to be highly suspicious. Yet without such goals and objectives how can there be any way of measuring how far we might have come down the road to justice, let alone present a horizon for which to aim? There is no doubt then that the human rights discourse includes a powerful messianic component and that this gives it some common ground or a possible location where a relationship with faith traditions might take place. Do we share a similar vision for the future of the planet and its peoples? If not, how would ours differ and what practical differences would this make? These are some of the questions that might form an ongoing conversation.

2. The universal and the particular in human rights

The language of human rights stands firmly within the Enlightenment tradition and thus claims to be of universal significance. Whatever forms in which they are constructed the intention is that such rights are applicable across national and cultural boundaries. However, the reality is that they derive from a very specific set of historical circumstances and do contain significant differences. So, for instance, the statements issuing from the French Revolution, then from the American Constitution and then from the 1948 Declaration of Human Rights are each key elements in the development of this discourse. They are particular in their background and subsequent articulation and interpretation. On what grounds then can they legitimately claim to be universal?

A further obvious complication is that the human rights tradition is essentially a by-product of Western liberal democracy and is perceived by some who stand outside that tradition to be a political tool of the major Western powers, especially the USA and the European Union. How are other nations and other cultures to relate to this set of ideas? Any claim to neutrality is now likely to be dismissed as unjustified in the light of the postmodern critique of grand narratives and the unveiling of the Enlightenment tradition as just one more ideology. Faith traditions thus stand alongside other cultural and political traditions in having to decide how much of the human rights discourse is consistent with their beliefs and practices. Yet the need for some sort of global code of behaviour becomes ever more evident and even if this particular movement is not going to be the one to address that need then something similar will surely be required. So perhaps it is not that the tension between particular and universal can ever be resolved in favour of one or the other, but rather that this tension is an inescapable and necessary component of the search for a transcontextual or global code of practice. Despite being particular and derived from a very specific culture and intellectual tradition, human rights are, as yet, the only real candidate for a foundation for a global ethic.

However, there is another tension that must be recognized within the human rights discourse. Although human rights now take the form of legislation either at a national or transnational level, it is in practice only at the most local level that they take on any reality. There is no 'universal humanity' which is the subject of human rights, but only particular individuals or groups of people who live in a particular place at a particular time. As with any legislation there will always be the questions of implementation and interpretation. What does this statement of human rights mean in practice in this specific situation? Migrant workers who feel themselves to be exploited by gangmasters who are knowingly flouting the laws of their own country will want to know how – if at all – they can be protected by human rights legislation. If they cannot, then the discourse is simply a set of words and fine intentions that makes no earthly difference to their lives. If this tension sounds familiar for faith traditions then so it should! Words are empty unless they can be translated into action here and now. Talk about caring for the other who is in need is of no use in itself, it needs to be incarnated.

A further aspect of this is that governments and international agencies have now appropriated the language of human rights and turned it into another set of codes and criteria (the Saying has become the Said). It was invariably the experiences of particular individuals that created the need for something like human rights and it was invariably governments and their agencies which were responsible for their infringements. This is surely a case of poacher turned gamekeeper. There is now a massive human rights 'industry', one might argue, with many professionals earning their livings off the back of it, probably doing their best for their clients but often at one remove from the original experiences. The singularities are once again submerged beneath the processes of articulation and political necessity; the ideals are in constant danger of disappearing beneath a tidal wave of paperwork and bureaucracy. Yet how can those singularities enter the public world and make a wider difference unless there is such articulation? Can one witness in silence to human rights?

Finally, there is the constant danger of particular nations employing the discourse of human rights as a way of justifying acting on its own political or economic agenda. The war against Iraq in 2003 is a clear case in point. The contravention of the human rights of the people of Iraq was certainly presented as one justification for the invasion, although the invaders had also played an ambiguous role in that and some argued that their use of sanctions did as much damage as the country's own internal regime. It is impossible to settle the rights and wrongs of this particular case, but the risk is that employing the language in this sort of way will devalue it and lead only to suspicion and cynicism. If it is simply a blind for action taken for other reasons then it will fail to carry any weight with those peoples who might otherwise have trusted in it and gained some benefit from it. Yet perhaps this is part of the indeterminacy and uncertainty of political life and what will inevitably happen to ideals once they enter the political arena. The wider point though is that the tension between universal and particular that I have identified as being a potential location for the relationship between reason and faith is clearly recognizable in this instance.

3. The subject within human rights

The major problem in this respect are the definitions that have to be presented in order to categorize those individuals whose rights are to be protected in any particular instance. What are the particular characteristics that mean that this individual or group of people can be identified as in need of protection? There is obviously a range of possible answers. Is it women who are to be the subjects, or a specific group of women belonging to a class or nationality? Then there is a need for workers to be granted rights let alone refugees or the homeless. Rights are now being extended into areas of social and economic life and this is a matter of some controversy. Is there any aspect of human life that will not carry with it some sort of right before long? What is the point of creating rights that cannot actually be protected or translated into practical action? However, the issue for us is that of the categorization of human beings and the danger of thereby reducing individuals to particular sets of characteristics. What is being constructed through this use of language is effectively a 'legal subject', a fictional and partial being who bears less and less resemblance to a real person. Such definitions move ever closer to the Habermasian subject, a rational being who may indeed have aspects of their being that escape description but since these cannot be put into language they are unable to be acknowledged within the human rights discourses. Once again one is moving away from the singularity or uniqueness of the individual human being, that which was initially in need of being protected against political and bureaucratic tendencies to categorize and potentially oppress. The unconscious, the affective and emotional, all that defies articulation may not be brought into the domain of rights but yet may be the most powerful basis for a critique of current practice. Is this to lose sight of the 'other' who should be the real subject of human rights? Douzanis seems to suggest that this is so:

> The demand of the other and my obligation to respond are the 'essence' of the ethics of alterity. But this 'essence' is based on the non-essence of the other who cannot be turned into the instance of a concept, the application of a law or the particularization of the universal ego.   (Douzanis 2000, 350)

What is required is an understanding of human subjectivity that can do justice to those other dimensions already mentioned, perhaps not just the pre-autonomous dimension but what rests beyond autonomy. This we will return to in later chapters having merely noted here that this is indeed another area where both faith and reason have a conversation to pursue.

4. Democracy, indeterminacy and human rights

A straightforward question comes to mind at this point. How much can actually be achieved and how much changed merely by creating the legislation that is now the backbone of human rights? Making laws and placing ideals on the statute books is only one aspect of what is required. It is behaviour, attitudes and prevalent practices that need to change if people's rights are to be respected. Even within a democratic system, and even within one that adheres to the inclusivity advocated by Habermas, there are no guarantees that people will play by those rules. Creating charters and issuing grand statements of intent may have symbolic value and may indeed be steps on the way to changing attitudes and practices, but they are not a substitute for genuine change. The indeterminacy of political life and the influence of the decisions that politicians and leaders make in the heat of the day will always counteract the best of intentions. These will be a limiting factor upon the ideals of human rights just as they will be upon those of any faith tradition. The temptation to imagine that putting deeds into words and ideals into legislation will create the kingdom of God, or any other messianic concept, must be resisted. No one political structure will be able to do justice to the vision that lies behind the human rights discourses. So here is the final area where faith and reason may have much to debate and share.

Conclusion

The claim at this stage must be modest. I would argue that identifying these four locations as of potential significance for the pursuit of the relationship between reason and faith is a step on a journey and no more. However, if the cultural schizophrenia that seems to divide faith from public life is to be addressed and corrected, then this is at least a move in the right direction. There is enough of shared understanding and concern to warrant further exploration and one can see this from the brief examination of the key area of human rights. However, more examination is now required and for this I will return to the grounding in local, practical activity and introduce a further set of theoretical resources.

4

Happy families

Introduction

This story begins on a summer's evening, on 5 June 2000 to be precise. I was attending a Parochial Church Council meeting of one of my four parishes prior to starting a period of study leave. We were talking about our children's work within the area, and, in particular, how to encourage greater contact with a number of young families who had recently moved onto a new estate in the main centre of population. It was one of those moments when inspiration struck two of us at exactly the same time. A former parishioner and churchwarden had been talking about a Children's Festival run by his new parishes. This consisted of a day devoted to activities for children up to ten years old, organized and run by the local churches and with some Christian content as well as community involvement. I looked over at one of our Sunday school teachers, and we said to one another 'we must run our own Children's Festival'. Having said that of course, we really had no idea what we meant by this, let alone how we would do it or what it would involve. If it was to be then it would be. It was our shared view that there was a need here to be met and that this might be one way of addressing it. In this way are crazy but ultimately fruitful schemes brought to birth. It was a moment of madness in that I was just about to start three months off work and the last thing that I should sensibly do was to set another project running. However, it did prove to be a turning point.

Four days later I was visiting the local playgroup and talking to some of the mums in the Mothers and Toddlers' room and happened to mention this idea. One of the mums immediately said that what we needed to do to was to form a committee. She took a piece of paper and sent it around the room asking other mums to sign up for the Children's Festival committee. Most of them signed, again without any real notion of what we were talking about or what they might be getting into and, from that morning, we had the basis of the organizing group. Thinking back to that day, which now seems very distant, three of those families are now part of our own church-based Mothers and Toddlers group, which is what has evolved from the Festival. Two of those families are also now involved in the local church-aided school governing body and there are now eight families from the not-so-new estate who regularly attend our twice-monthly Toddlers group. Perhaps it was not such a crazy idea after all.

I will return to aspects of the story as we go along. However, I want to offer some initial reflections on how and why this story fits into my wider picture. It strikes me that I could have begun this account in exactly the same way as I did the first chapter, by talking about the couple who turned up on my doorstep in 1987 looking for a house to rent. This is so because part of my involvement with and concern for this new housing development was the provision of a number of dwellings for rent, hopefully for local families. My initial motivation for going on the Board of the newly-formed Housing Association was precisely because I knew there was going to be an estate of 58 properties built in the middle of my patch and, because of my previous experience in Shropshire, I wanted to try to exert some influence over what type of properties were constructed. For those not familiar with the regulations, most District Council planning departments will put what is known as a 'Section 106 order' on developments of this sort, insisting that a proportion of the properties will be let at an affordable rent. In other words, they will belong to a Housing Association. I wanted to try to ensure that the 10% regulation, i.e. 6 properties on the new development, were indeed destined for our Housing Association if at all possible. Again, looking back, this did happen, although it now no longer seems a major theme of this particular story. But there was, at the beginning, a housing need dimension to this involvement and wider issues about house prices, mortgages and lifestyles of families will impinge in due course.

All of this is to say that I could have begun the story at another point in time and with a different set of encounters. I do think it is important to recognize this. It is sometimes assumed that the method of 'telling the story', of offering a narrative which provides the way into further debate, is privileged over other possible methods. I am 'telling it the way it is', and therefore there is an immunity from criticism or counter interpretations. This cannot be the case. I am acutely conscious that the accounts I will offer could be presented in a number of different ways and even with conflicting views on what any of this means. The model that I have is that of a kaleidoscope. In order to present a coherent account and to allow a pattern to emerge I have to stop turning the kaleidoscope and allow a picture to settle and be observed. Wherever I choose to stop it, I know that I could equally well have chosen to stop it somewhere else and then the patterns might look very different. Perhaps we are back once again with Levinas's tension between the Saying and the Said. The accounts have to be articulated in order for myself and others to encounter and respond to them. Yet there are always things lost in that process. The Saying, the initial human encounters, and also sometimes the ideas that inspire and stimulate, may be hidden beneath the apparent detail. Whether or not a particular articulation of the story is a distortion, or to what extent it does justice to the events, is perhaps only for others to judge. One can only offer the disclaimer that this is one version of what happened and that others could also be told. There may even be aspects that cannot by their very nature be fully articulated, a Saying that, like Abraham's encounter with God, escapes the confines of language. Most of us can only tell or relate to one story at a time.

I also reflect that there are elements of continuity with the practical engagements which formed the basis for *Local Theology*. Although I am now working in a quite different context and have been here for a considerably longer period of time, the same three core issues have arisen. They are those of housing provision, work with families and children and finally environmental concerns. I draw no conclusions from this. I assume that colleagues who are similarly involved in community activities and projects may also tend to veer towards the same type of concerns in different settings. I can only imagine that our own personal commitments and contacts are inevitably an influence upon and a factor in what will happen in any given situation. This is the particular at work again even within the wider transcontextual setting of the church. There is a personal Saying as there will always be particular local issues that call forth a response.

Finally though, before I return to the story, there is another aspect of that earlier work that also continues to resonate with the current experience. The idea of the Poppy Seed Head as an image for doing local theology is still the model which best describes my own experience. In other words, from an initial idea or encounter, activities and reflections explode out in any number of different directions and then cannot neatly be contained and drawn back into a theoretical system. This has implications for the resources or frameworks of interpretation on which I need to draw. No single set of resources can do the job simply because the reality that I encounter is complex, multi-layered and constantly shifting. Any one involvement, even that as apparently straightforward as working with children and young families, will lead to a series of problematics or set of issues around a particular theme. Therefore the resources that could be used to help analyse and interpret these problematics will themselves be plural and complex. This makes for an inescapably complex business and for difficulty in reducing 'the story' to a tight set of events and reflections. Also, somebody else could well approach the same set of issues very differently. Thus are our encounters blurred by all of the particular, personal and contextual dimensions of our involvements. For those who feel more comfortable with explicit theological terminology, I would say that this is part of the cost of incarnation. It is about taking the complexities of our lives seriously.

Children's Festival 2001

Almost exactly twelve months after the initial idea was born our first Children's Festival took place. We located the event in the local village hall in the largest centre of population in the parishes and also hired a large marquee. Having said that we would cater for a maximum of 75 children, including a workshop for pre-school age children with a carer present, we ended up with over 80 children attending. During the day we ran a number of workshops staffed by a mixture of church-based leaders and professional community-based artists, each group also having a number of adult helpers present. It would take too long to describe the events of the day and one can never capture the excitement generated, but one of my abiding memories will be the looks of pleasure on the children's faces as we said farewell to them at 3.00 p.m. We knew that they had had a good day and that all the hard work had been worth it. Twelve months of planning, almost monthly meetings of one sort or another including applying for and getting a grant from the National Lottery, which set us free to employ the people we needed, had paid off. Rather than going into all the details of this what I want to do is to highlight key issues that arose during the process and then to illustrate how they inform our wider debate about the blurring of boundaries drawing upon some theoretical resources. As I have already said, many other places have run such Festivals so the idea was not original, but what will be more particular is the context in which this was set and the ways in which we went about the activity.

Before I move on to this I simply want to state my own principle of operation which spans much of my work at a parish level. I see a fundamental part of my role as either discerning or creating locations for encounter. In other words, it is up to me to find opportunities to enable other people to cross the boundary into the world of the Christian tradition whether this involves encountering ideas or, perhaps more likely, the people who represent that tradition. Call this mission if you like, but I would not use that term in the narrow sense of conversion but in the wider sense of encounter. For me, the Children's Festival was an attempt to create a location for encounter and to see what might happen when people were prepared to enter a different space. For parents, children and even the organizing committee it was about providing a memorable and enjoyable community event for the children. But it would also hopefully be of value for the adults involved. In terms of numbers, this meant that, by the end of the day, including the adults who came to share in the closing ceremony, about 150 people had taken part. For parishes with a total population of just over 1000 this seems reasonable.

In order to access the Lottery grant we needed to establish ourselves as a community group and to create a constitution. This is always a good exercise because it enables the group to monitor their own progress and evaluate their success. Our stated objectives were as follows. To hold a one day Children's Festival for children

aged 0–10 years and their families from the local community; for children to participate in a variety of creative activities; for participating adults to be able to develop
new skills and enhance existing ones; to promote and develop closer links between
local community groups including the school, the local playgroup and parent and
toddlers group, and the church-based Sunday school. The first two of these would
be obvious objectives, but perhaps the second two are the more significant. We
envisaged the process of creating the Festival as itself an opportunity for the personal
development of the adults involved. This was not just about the children, although
the final event was clearly primarily for them. In broad idealistic terms, who might
we become or what might we each discover about ourselves and one another during
the course of this process? In classic community work or adult education terms,
this was a journey or a pilgrimage leading to a particular goal, but the journey itself
was of significance. The key aspect to be aware of is that the organizing committee
included both the slightly older generation of parents who had been in the locality
for some years and some younger parents who had recently moved into the area and
needed to find their own way into the 'community'. So this was a potential crossing
of boundaries between 'locals' and 'newcomers' as well as between church and
non-church and indeed between two generations. This links clearly with the final
objective, that of developing closer links between different groups in the area.

Some description of the local context is required if one is to understand why
this was so important. The four separate parishes of which I am priest-in-charge
are located between Droitwich and Kidderminster, about 20 miles south-east of
Birmingham and 10 minutes away from the M5. They are rural only in the sense that
they are small communities and that farming is still a feature of the area, although
only as a fragment of the whole, not as a dominant factor. Although there has been
some movement in the population over time, what I encountered when I arrived
in 1992 was a fairly static and established set of relationships both in church and
wider community. I learnt before too long that there was a proposal to build a new
estate of 58 houses in the largest centre of population in the parishes – hence my
concern about the provision of affordable housing as part of this. What was then
unknown was who was likely to move into these houses, what age groups we would
be looking at and, of course, the possibility of people there being drawn into and
getting involved in existing community activities. For these parishes, the prospect
of quite a substantial influx of new people meant an encounter with the 'unknown
other' and all the fears and challenges that this would represent. For myself as parish
priest it meant the challenge of creating locations for encounter and trying to bridge
the differences between possibly diverse groups and expectations. The Children's
Festival needs to be seen in that context of 'encountering the other'.

As it happened, a significant number of young families moved into this new
estate, along with a more predictable number of older and retired people. This

would be potentially important for the local school (a Voluntary Aided school with key church involvement) and indeed for all the other branches of children's work in the area including the playgroup, the Sunday school and our monthly family service. My own guess and indeed fear was that we would manage only a minimal level of contact with such families because of the obvious issues of lifestyle and lack of church background. This would not be 'fertile' territory for 'mission'! However, the task and the challenge was there, not just for me but for all the existing groups and church congregations. Looking back now since the first people moved onto the estate in 1998 I have been pleasantly surprised by what has been achieved. Much of this is down to the fact that certain families on the estate already had a church background and were keen to become involved and to work at drawing others in with them. We were extremely fortunate in that respect, but the work still needed to be done and the opportunities created. From the original organizing committee for the Festival, four families lived on the new estate and another four were regular attenders at the local playgroup or Mothers and Toddlers session. Only three of us could be said to have a regular church commitment – at that time anyway.

Another aspect of the context that needs to be registered is that I had found it almost impossible to generate sustainable community activity of any description. This was not for want of trying. In the early days I had attempted to establish a community forum for discussion of matters of local concern working alongside a community worker. However, although this had identified key people who had a grasp of that approach, it quickly fell foul of the four parish councils who felt that we were impinging on their territory. As a result the group ran into the ground. My experience was that people were either too busy or else too comfortable to want to engage in anything beyond their immediate social life, some of which was church-based, but did not go much beyond the normal run of fund-raising events. So the prospects for the Festival were not good, unless the influx of new people and younger families could create a momentum for change. In fact, this is what has happened. The 'other' has successfully broken open the existing establishment and generated relationships and activities that could not have been foreseen, even by the ever-optimistic vicar! To employ some of the sociological terminology, how could we create actors out of bystanders and participators out of consumers? I think it can be claimed that we have had some limited success in this, although it is always particular local factors and key people who make this possible.

What of the local church's role in this? It has to be acknowledged that it was not always comfortable and certainly not clear-cut. I was very conscious from the outset that what might happen would simply be that we would create a new constituency or new group that would have its own identity and requirements. If this happened then the aim of integrating new people into the existing structures and thereby, hopefully, changing those structures, would not be achieved. From the early days of the Children's Festival it was clear that achieving a balance between creating a new group and making the links with existing ones such that they 'owned' what was happening was not going to be easy. I found myself talking up this proposed event and the promising contact with new young families for months before the occasion while it was clear that the established church groups did not really grasp the potential significance of what might happen. Of course, there was always a risk that it would not happen. We did not find out that we had the Lottery grant until March and it was only really once bookings started coming in towards the end of April that we felt we had a viable operation on our hands. We were working 'at risk' until then with all the dangers of shattered hopes and expectations should the event not take place. This was uncharted territory and for those involved a lot was at stake.

Although there was an 'in principle' support from the church councils, church members and the school for the Festival, it was difficult to describe to them precisely what might happen let alone whether or not it would be a success. There was certainly an issue over how much explicit Christian content there would be in the workshops. If the churches were 'hosting' this in some serious way, and if the vicar was spending so much time on this one event, should there not be an immediate and identifiable gain for the church, or, at least, a significant stake in terms of content? Yet, if this was to be a genuine community event, encouraging those who would not otherwise think of coming to anything 'churchy' to participate, how could it be presented in a way which they too would be comfortable with? I would have to say that I felt I had to shield the process from those who would have wanted too much 'heavy' religious content, while simultaneously arguing that the theme of Pentecost with its visual and imaginative aspects could be kept 'light' enough to not put off non-churchgoers. Even the workshop leaders we selected were potentially controversial. I used one friend from Shropshire days who is more of a Buddhist than a Christian and a children's worker from the Diocese of Hereford who, in a sense, represented the church establishment, but would also present 'faith' in an appropriately 'light' way. A couple of Diocesan officers from our own diocese were also involved, so it was a mixture and, hopefully one that would keep all sides happy. Inevitably though, we were crossing the boundary between church and non-church and this created its own tensions.

The main way by which we involved regular church attenders in the event was to recruit adult helpers for the day itself. This was crucial as we had committed ourselves to a one-to-five adult to child ratio as part of our adherence to good practice and to child protection guidelines. So we needed around twenty other adults who were not part of the organizing committee to work with us. This was where we had to draw on the congregations to get involved. Some were keen and others not, but we did get the support we needed. Having said that, there were elements of the organization on the day that could have been improved upon, but we did have the excuse that we had never done anything like this before. Taking responsibility for over 80 children and ensuring health and safety requirements, security and child protection is a major undertaking even when you have committee members with the appropriate skills and experience.

Once it was all over and there was the opportunity to reflect we conducted our own internal evaluation. What had we learnt from this and where might we go from here given its obvious success? The issue of explicit religious content came to the surface once again with the feeling being expressed that we had gone too far in that direction and that there were families who would not support it again on those grounds. Personally I found that frustrating when I felt I had tried to 'play down' that aspect of the day to the point where I was risking criticism from some key churchgoers. This is one of the risks of crossing the boundary: neither side may be completely convinced by what is on offer. Was this a compromise? Who was appropriating whom? Had we indeed 'eaten well' in this case or instead got a nasty dose of indigestion? Overall I would argue that the balance achieved was probably the best we could have done, but the issues remained.

What then happened is that we had to make a decision about whether or not we would run the event the following year. One major factor was that we had a reasonable sum of money left over from the Lottery grant, in addition to the residue of what other local groups had contributed. It was suggested that we repeat the event in 2 years time to give the committee a break, but I felt that momentum and interest would have been lost by then and, that if we were to keep the organizing committee together, we needed to aim for the same next year. That was what was agreed. Some committee members said that they no longer wished to be involved, which was perfectly understandable, but most of us were prepared to carry on. We felt that certain lessons had been learnt in terms of content and structure of the event and would be put into practice next time. So, we started planning for 2002.

Inevitably perhaps the Festival of 2002 did not seem to have quite the same edge and excitement. Although numbers attending were still healthy they were down on the previous year. Had the novelty worn off or had some stayed away because the event was too Christian? I suspect it was a bit of both. I deliberately stayed distant from the content of the workshops and left a sub-group to organize that. The result was that they moved towards the safer ground of children's entertainment rather than the more ambitious and risky community arts territory of the previous year. There was nothing wrong in this, but it did change the nature of the event in my view and in that of some of my church people. My conclusion after the Festival of 2002 was that it had achieved its original purpose and that life had now moved on – which it had in ways that I will describe shortly – and that enough was enough. We were not creating a tradition, but had run something memorable which was 'for the time being only'. Some of the boundaries had now been crossed, others remained firmly in place. However, from this initial location of encounter, new possibilities were to be born. Before moving on to consider these I now want to link this experience to some theoretical resources in order to illustrate how this particular local event can inform our thinking about wider issues.

Castells on the search for identity

One way of interpreting the familiar conflicts and negotiations between locals and newcomers is as an attempt to establish a cultural and individual identity. One defines who one is both in relationship to those around with whom one readily identifies but also in distinction to those whom one perceives as being different or other. This applies equally to the boundary between those who belong to a particular 'faith community' and to those who do not. Hence the issues underlying the question of the use of explicit religious material in the Children's Festivals are an aspect of this process. Was this a Christian or church-based event or not? How would one define that anyway and who would be concerned to do that defining? There were some on the church side of the divide who felt uneasy that the event was not Christian enough, just as there were some on the non-church side who felt that it was too explicitly Christian. There were others of us who were not so concerned to establish such clear boundaries and found this discussion frustrating and even unnecessary. However, there was no escaping the importance of these questions for each of the different groups involved. For the 'locals' there were, and still are, issues of who determines what happens in the area and for the 'newcomers' a concern to decide to what extent one can belong or buy into and then influence the culture of the locality.

In one sense these problems are nothing new and simply a matter of one group or individual encountering another and sorting out where one stands in relation to the 'other'. It is important though, I would argue, to recognize that there are those who argue that this search for identity is a reaction to the forces of globalization and now manifests itself in new and potentially disturbing ways. One such author is the sociologist Castells (Castells 1997) and it his work that I want to draw upon here. His argument is that the growing uncertainty, insecurity and pace of change created by the latest stages of the growth of global capitalism lead to a series of defensive reactions, one of which is the search to establish secure and clearly-bounded identities. I believe that there is enough truth in this to make it valuable as a framework of analysis in my particular context.

> Our world, and our lives, are being shaped by the conflicting trends of globalization and identity. The information technology revolution, and the restructuring of capitalism, have induced a new form of society, the network society. It is characterized by the globalization of strategically decisive economic activities. By the networking form of organization. By the flexibility and instability of work, and the individualization of labour.   (Castells 1997, 2)

What has also happened in the last thirty years is 'the widespread surge of powerful expressions of collective identity that challenge globalization and cosmopolitanism on behalf of cultural singularity and people's control over their lives and environment' (Castells 1997, 3). In other words, the stakes have been raised and the question of identity has become that much more significant. Castells is thinking particularly of movements such as feminism and the environmental lobby, but also of forms of religious fundamentalism and growing ethnic and nationalistic tendencies. When one perceives oneself to be under threat from an external 'other', the temptation is always to retreat behind the barricades and insist that everybody must be either 'one of us' or 'one of them'. This requires the clear and decisive drawing of boundaries and establishing of criteria. The fear of losing control, of being consumed or appropriated by the 'other' leads one to a defensive reaction and the search for a clear identity. So it is not surprising that 'locals' who feel under threat from the invasion by an alien culture, in this case one with 'money to burn' and all the trappings of affluence, rapidly resent the presence of newcomers and their potential impact upon 'their' community. Similarly some Christians who abide by a strict definition of their faith, often based upon the authority of Scripture, feel uneasy when others suggest a more critical approach!

Castells's ideas have further implications that are important for this discussion. He is interested in the formation of what he calls a 'primary identity', that which gives meaning to a person's life on the basis of a set of cultural attributes. Although such identities can be the result of external institutions such as a religious or political grouping, it is increasingly the case that they are formed outside such institutions as individuals are thrown back on their own resources to construct their sense of themselves. If we feel that our choices in determining who we might be or become are being restricted by external forces we are now likely to interpret this as a lack of freedom or personal choice, even as a violation of our 'rights'. In this context Castells suggests that there are three forms and origins of identity building.

First there is a 'legitimizing identity'. This is where one determines oneself primarily in relationship to an external body or institution, for instance that of a faith community. So one establishes one's identity by making it clear that one conforms to the accepted norms of personality and behaviour as set out by that body. Belonging to any social grouping, even being a supporter of a particular football team, can have that effect. Second there is a 'resistance identity' where those who feel threatened in some way by external forces gather in 'community' to form close bonds and boundaries in order to protect themselves against uncertainty. Then finally there is what Castells calls 'project identity', where people consciously attempt to establish new and changed identities not simply as a defence but as a positive force for change, thus some feminists strive for a redefinition of both male and female being.

Each of these forms of identity building is of wider political significance. Legitimating identity operates within what political theorists term civil society, those areas of our lives that stand between formal politics and major institutions and that which is seen as private and personal. So churches and voluntary groups are part of civil society. A number of thinkers have believed that civil society is the most effective site of opposition to unacceptable political structures. However, Castells does not appear to share this view. Resistance identity, he argues, leads to the formation of 'communes' or 'communities' in the sense of tight-knit and even fundamentalist groupings and can only add to the growing fragmentation of social and political life. The major problem with such 'communities' is that they are unwilling to talk to one another simply because they have to be 'right' and everybody else is then 'wrong'. However, some resistance identities do appear to have the capacity to encourage and nurture the formation of project identities. I believe that a vital question for Christian communities is that of which ones and under what conditions?

This framework parallels some thoughts of my own on the nature of religious identity. I have long thought that religion's effects on individuals are either legitimating, i.e. supporting a status quo; integrating – giving people a sense of belonging or community; or critical, encouraging a questioning and forward-looking approach to life. Given that much of the community based work in which I have been engaged, and I count the Children's Festival in this category, is integrating or creating Castell's resistance identity, I wonder what possibilities exist for this becoming the base for a more critical or project identity approach. This seems to me to highlight the problem or limitations of the events which churches currently organize. What often attracts people is the sense of belonging to and being part of an identifiable social group, a group which then defines itself by contrast with those who are 'other' or different. The risks of becoming exclusive and excluding are considerable. Integration does indeed take place but at the cost of that response to those who are different that is a vital aspect of the Christian faith. If Castells is correct in arguing that these tendencies are enhanced by the alien forces of globalization and the consequent threats to both family and community stability, then churches are even more prone to encouraging the creation of resistance identities. Close-knit, temporary networks, often based on communities of interest rather than necessarily upon locality or class, become highly attractive propositions, relying upon the development of trust or intimacy that is the more intense for being temporary. The possibility that people will move away from the locality for reasons of work or lifestyle choice alters the dynamic from that of previous communities where people could be expected to remain for thirty or forty years. For the sake of coining a phrase I term this the creation of 'enclaves of interim intimacy'. A number of churches are now in this business in one way or another.

Now while this is not necessarily wrong in itself, if it does lead to enclosed communities and a purely defensive reaction to external pressures, then it has to be brought into question. It may be the beginning of a journey towards 'faith', but the risk is that the journey ends there out of either comfort or inertia, and the further stage is never even glimpsed let alone attained. How do we turn resistance identities into project identities? That I think is the challenge which Castells throws down to us, and rightly so. It is clear that this is not simply a local question, but one that has significant global implications. Resistance identity is at the heart of those wider political and religious groupings that, when taken to the extreme, threaten peace and stability. There are those who would want to say that religion can only encourage the formation of closed or fundamentalist identities and is thus to be resisted and kept out of public life. If one wants to challenge this one must offer examples to the contrary, not just at national but at local level. That is why the pressure is on such accounts as ours to show how it might be possible to build upon our community-based work to encourage the formation of a more critical or project identity. I want to keep this question in mind as I move on to the next stage of the local story.

The demise of the playgroup

One of the primary objectives of the Festival was to draw together and thus support the various strands of children's work within the parishes. A shared concern was that there was a worrying degree of fragmentation between the different enterprises and that combating this would be of benefit to all. So, for instance, having a healthy playgroup was important for the local school as well as being a central point of contact for the vicar who then stood a better chance of drawing families into church activities. Thus the continued existence of the playgroup was of wider significance. Remember also that forming the committee for the Festival happened at the Mothers and Toddlers section of the playgroup and that, without that, the event would not have taken place. It had been clear to me as soon as I arrived in the parishes that visiting this facility was an important part of my role and a vital point of contact with this age group. At the time of the formation of the Festival committee I was dropping into the group every Friday morning and spending time both with the playgroup and with the toddlers and mums. Over time this was starting to pay off as relationships of trust began to build. It was particularly significant because some of the new families from the estate were using this and it was becoming their main point of social contact, not only with one another, but also with the wider community. It was one of those classic cases of an investment of time starting to pay dividends and to generate other pieces of work.

The background to the playgroup was that it was formed by a number of local mothers of my generation during the late 1980s when their own children required that facility. It was locally based, small-scale, initially run by volunteers and yet important within the community. Some of those mothers subsequently used this experience to develop their own careers in this general area and also 'graduated' to becoming governors at the local school and indeed the more senior members of the Children's Festival committee. Hence there was both continuity and ownership of the group within the wider area by those who had a history with it. As these mums and their children moved on so others came in and took over, invariably those with their own young children. The viability of playgroup was seriously threatened by the voucher scheme for school places introduced by the Conservative government in the mid-1990s. This meant that the top end of the group – 4 year olds – would be 'creamed off' by the school and that numbers would be adversely affected. As Chair of school governors at the time I was in a difficult position, both having to put into place a school policy that would damage the playgroup and trying to support the playgroup perceiving itself to be under threat from the school. This was one of the reasons for the fragmentation mentioned earlier as, up until that point, there had been very good relations between the two, with frequent visits in both directions and a policy that the playgroup was the natural 'feed-in' to the school. However, we had no local control over this as it was government policy to offer parents more choices and to encourage the growth of childcare to enable more women to return to work. Subsequent government policies have continued this same approach and thus determined the wider context of this local work.

At the point at which the Festival began to take shape numbers and morale at the playgroup were reasonably good, particularly with the influx of new families. However, underlying issues were not really being addressed. The fairly low-key and ad hoc management of the group's finances and staffing policies that had been adequate for earlier years were starting to see signs of strain. In particular, as more and more playgroups became OFSTED registered and their staff more highly qualified and professionalized, there was a resistance within this group against moving in that direction. The parents who had recently moved into the area demanded a rather higher standard of provision and were already starting to look at the nurseries in the surrounding towns. This was a growing source of tension among the parents and even on the management committee itself and I was aware of some of the arguments that were going on behind the scenes. My feelings on this were ambivalent. I both wanted to continue to support the group because of its contribution over the years but also to encourage it to move towards the level at which it would retain the interest of the majority of mothers within the locality. This was also crucial for the school, because the more children who were taken to nurseries or playgroups outside the parish the greater the likelihood that they might make their friends and contacts there and not feed back into the local school when the time came to move on. All of us as school governors and staff were conscious of this threat to our numbers as well. So we were all of us in a difficult position with conflicts between our personal and structural commitments.

During and after the first Festival a number of cracks in the relationships began to appear, particularly between the locals who had put considerable time and energy into the playgroup and some of the newcomers who were keen to exercise choice and obtain the best services that they could for their children. I felt this also as a tension between a commitment to the locality and a commitment to get the best for one's own family even at the expense of undermining local provision. I asked myself what I would do in this situation if I had children at pre-school age. Would I feel that I had to support the local provision even if I was unhappy with it and knew that my children would get better attention elsewhere, or would I walk away from it and do what I thought was right for my children regardless of the impact upon the locality and its other children's work? There are no easy answers to this type of question and I know that all of the mothers, whichever side of the divide they ended up on, were conscious of this dilemma and often felt bad about whichever decision they made.

It was becoming clear by the time of the second Children's Festival that something was going to give before long. Both numbers and finances at the playgroup were starting to dwindle and there was real concern about its viability. There was a growing sense that it was moving towards a close and a sense of help-lessness to do anything about that or to see what would come next. The school was particularly concerned because of the potential impact upon its numbers and the fact that increasingly we were learning that local families were taking their children to other schools where there was on-site nursery provision and sometime before- and after-school clubs as well. I had a further concern which was that, having invested considerable time in building contact with the young families and run two Festivals, all of this could now count for nothing as the parents drifted away into the local towns for children's care and facilities. A further problem was the physical condition of the hall where the playgroup met, which left a lot to be desired and for which their management committee had tried and failed to get grants for rebuilding. I knew that some parents were unhappy to bring their very young children into a room that was often damp and difficult to heat.

What happened next will be the subject of the next chapter, but I do need to say that, up until this point, my policy had been to support the existing groups in the community if I possibly could rather than to start up my own church-based groups. This was one way in which I could continue to foster contact with non-church members and, in any case, we did not really have the resources and numbers to establish our own facilities in competition with what was already there. The playgroup had been an effective and important location for encounter and a means of reaching a constituency that I could not otherwise access. All of this was about to change. The playgroup did finally close at Christmas 2002 but, by then, I had already taken steps to ensure that the work we had begun would be continued. It was a sad moment, but circumstances change, giving us however much cause for reflection. Once again I now want to draw on some theory in order to illuminate what was happening in this part of the story.

Beck on individualisation

As I have just said, I felt this particular conflict acutely as part of a wider question about the tendency in our culture to place issues of individual choice and preference above those of collective concern and responsibility. If I was faced with a choice between supporting my local school or doing what I thought was best for my child, what would I do? I would probably feel that I had to do what was best for my child despite feeling residual guilt about the possible consequences of my actions for other people. A number of politicians let alone clergy find themselves struggling with similar questions and often deciding in exactly that way. Yet as parish priest and school governor I would always want to support the local provision and work towards its improvement and to encourage others to do the same. So what is this now about our culture that places so much importance upon individual choice?

There is a tendency in Christian circles to label this as a growing individualism and the victory of the 'me generation' over concern for the wider good. I am not convinced that it is quite as simple as that and I want to refer to the work of the German sociologist Ulrich Beck in order to reflect more deeply upon this (Beck and Beck-Gernsheim 2002). Once again we find ourselves in the general area of identity construction and of responses to wider political and economic changes that are now shaping our lives.

One of the words that captures so much that we now experience is 'indeterminacy'. I encounter this regularly in the lives of my parishioners. I think of the family on the new estate who were just starting to settle into the area with children at the school and attending Sunday school, also involved initially in the Children's Festival until the point where the husband's firm was taken over by an American company and suddenly he was faced with the choice of either re-locating to France or losing his job. They chose to relocate and we lost a committed family. Others are constantly facing similar decisions. How is it possible to create stability and continuity in our personal lives and therefore collective commitment when nobody knows what tomorrow may bring and where one might have to move to? This is the world of rapid and unforeseeable change that is the backdrop to this story. What happens to ordinary people as a result of this and what resources can we draw upon to help us cope with such levels of indeterminacy?

What Beck helpfully points out is that this is not individualism in the old sense of a self-sufficient person consciously directing and ordering their life according to some carefully worked-out personal plan, based on some notion of autonomy. It is what he calls institutional individualism driven by external forces such as the global economy, in the face of which we are constantly being forced to redraw the boundaries of our identity and to redefine our lives at a moment's notice, but without access to the institutional resources of politics, religion and family that used to shape our sense of self. We are thrown back on our own resources in order to create what he calls 'bricolage biographies', using new networks and alliances that are formed quickly and may have to be abandoned just as quickly. The old idea of a linear personal narrative where one could track one's life through various predictable stages, e.g. school, college, marriage, family, career with one company, grandchildren, retirement, death, no longer holds good. So human identity is not a 'given' but a task, one in which we are responsible for our own performances and also have to live with a sense of failure when things go wrong. The established traditions survive, but only in a residual manner as potential resources upon which one might choose to draw at a particular point in one's journey. But then, one might well choose not to draw upon them and that, in itself, changes their status in the task of identity construction. The idea that an individual is in control of their own life in contrast with the suggestion that their life is being shaped by the external forces of an established tradition is not what Beck is talking about here.

The vexed area of pension provision is a good example of this. The days when one's organization or employer set this all up and took responsibility are numbered, It is increasingly up to individuals to decide what to do and to make their own provision. Employees decide not to buy into the firm's pension scheme on the basis that they will be moving on within a couple of years or that their job may no longer exist. One takes the decision to move to a particular locality on the grounds that it has a good school and that there will be no more building in the years to come. But these expectations can turn out to be mistaken. It is not taken for granted that one will send one's child to the local village school because we are told we must now exercise choice and do what is best for our own child. If we get it wrong, we take the responsibility and our children may turn this against us in due course. We are forced into being consumers of services and having to live with the consequences of our decisions as there is no safety net there to catch us when we fall. We are condemned to activity, to making up our lives as we go along, to taking the risks and paying the price of failure. Any decisions we make may seem as though they are 'until further notice only'. We decide to take this course of action 'for the time being' until circumstances or our minds are changed.

I can recognize so much of this from my own life and from that of my children let alone my parishioners. It leaves real questions for local church and community as to how we operate effectively in this context. Do we go along with these tendencies and adapt our worship and collective activity accordingly, or do we try to hold the line and to present an alternative order of things still based on continuity and stability? Do we really have a choice in the matter? I will return to some of these issues in the next chapter.

For the moment I want to point out that what happened with our local playgroup and the decisions that were subsequently made can only be understood against the backdrop of this rapidly changing and indeterminate context. Our culture is one where we are forced into making important choices about our lives without being able to rely in the old way on the stable and familiar resources of previous generations. Rather than simply one tradition or source of guidance being available to us there are now a number and this changes the nature of our relationship with those traditions. Even when we do choose to use those resources it is still a choice that we have to make and we have to live with the possibility that we have got it wrong or that we might have to make a different choice tomorrow. That destabilizes much that the old institutions normally try to do and some will go to the wall as a consequence. We are being forced across the boundary into a world driven by global economic and political forces and over which we have little or no control. So how are we to respond to this new situation?

5

The birth of Toddlers

New beginnings

By the start of 2002 it was clear that the playgroup and therefore also the Mothers and Toddlers session which had been the location for encounter with the young families was beginning to disintegrate. I could see all the work of the previous two years coming to nothing as I lost contact with the new families with the added risk that they would also drift away from the school and other local activities. I had to remind myself that there were such things as pram services and that it was possible for churches to run their own groups for toddlers and parents. The thought of this filled me with apprehension as it was not the sort of thing I had ever been involved in or had any wish to do. In addition it compromised my long-standing policy not to set up internal church groups when they already existed out in the community. However, this time around I could not see any alternative. I could at least try it and, if it failed, then I would have done the best I could. If I did nothing the contact would certainly be lost. As with the idea for the Children's Festival, it sort of turned up in my mind one day and I felt that I had to pursue it.

I went to see one of the mothers who had been part of the Children's Festival committee to float the idea and see what support there might be. We could think of four or five families who might form a core constituency for a monthly meeting and that seemed to be enough to make it worth starting. I also spoke to the Diocesan Children's Officer about how to run one of these things, what resources were required, where to meet and so on. None of our churches are large enough to provide the space for this so we approached one of the recently rebuilt church halls and made a monthly booking for a Thursday morning on the grounds that we judged this might be the best timing for the group. It was the beginning of February and we planned our first meeting for the following month. I was aware that this would create tensions with the existing playgroup as it struggled to survive and that I did not want to present this as setting up in opposition to them, even though it was inevitably going to have that effect. I continued to visit the playgroup faithfully on a Friday morning until its ultimate demise at the end of 2002. As I mentioned this germ of an idea to some of the other mothers, one of them who had the professional skills to run this sort of activity immediately volunteered to get involved and we rapidly drew in some others to establish an informal organizing committee. We did not anticipate large numbers attending but there were at least enough to make it worthwhile and I decided to use some funding I had from the local trust to purchase some necessary equipment. As I write this I can remember the mixture of apprehension and excitement that accompanied the early stages of this project. Would anybody turn up? What would I have organized for the toddlers let alone their mothers if and when they arrived? How was I supposed to work with this very young age group for which I had received no training? Despite the fact that I was an experienced parish priest, this was uncharted territory and I was concerned about starting a new area of work. Fortunately the mothers had a much better idea about what should happen and quickly realized that the vicar needed organizing and the group began to take shape. We were learning as we went along, reflecting constantly on how we should do things differently or better and refining the structures and activities. The crucial thing was to create a welcoming and safe environment and a place where both children and mothers felt secure and comfortable and could enjoy each other's company and support. In one sense it just happened to be run by the church, with the vicar as one of the prime movers and therefore would contain some light religious content. So this is what we did and it began to work.

What issues arose as we made this new beginning? Clearly the question of how to handle the explicit religious content – given that this was a church-based group – was on our agenda from the start. With the Children's Festival we had encountered opposition to making the content too religious, so would we immediately alienate or exclude families who were not comfortable or familiar with the Christian tradition? Was this simply going to be a small enclosed group for the few who already had a church grounding? What was our identity going to be? That is one set of issues. Another was that of how we related this group to the existing church constituency. Would this just be a small enclave whose only real connection with the church was the vicar, especially as we chose not to meet in the church but in the hall as both a more substantial and a more neutral space? How successful could we hope to be in terms of numbers given that so many mothers went back to work on a full or part time basis and were just not around consistently enough to attend a daytime activity? Would the pressures of lifestyle, demands of the global economy and subsequent problems for family and community life militate against this kind of group, or could we actually be a support for those who were subject to these pressures? Then there was still the underlying tension between locals and newcomers that had haunted the Children's Festival. The ailing playgroup was closely identified with the locals whereas this new group was built very much upon the newcomers to the area and families from the new estate, so was our activity going to be divisive and exacerbate those differences?

Then there was the question of professionalism. Given that the waning popularity of the existing playgroup was certainly partly due to their resistance to the demands of new mothers to provide a higher standard of care and activity, what pressures would we face to offer something more professional, thus competing with properly run nursery facilities? Could we deliver this? Finally there was the issue of the personal and professional development of the committee members themselves and whether – like the Children's Festival – this could be a location for encounter with a wider set of ideas and challenges. So there was immediately a great deal at stake in this new project and, of course, the risk of failure should the group not succeed or the opposing unknown demands of success should the group prove to have been the appropriate way forward.

What I want to do now is to describe the development of the group as it relates to those particular issues. In each instance we were faced with the crossing or the blurring of boundaries and of deeper underlying questions of how 'faith' could have both a practical and intellectual impact upon this most basic area of human activity, that of nurturing young children and supporting their parents. This is work still very much in progress, so the story can only be told from where we are now, just over two years into the project. The future holds further questions for us.

A Christian identity?

From the very beginning the question of how to handle the explicit Christian dimension of this project has continued to pose dilemmas for us. Given that this was to be a church-based operation as distinct from the existing playgroup the religious content was one way of justifying what we were about to do. The old model of a pram service was certainly at the back of this, but the fact that it was more appropriate to meet in the village hall and that we wanted to extend our activities beyond the obvious 'service' part of the session to include social time for mothers and play time for the children left a question mark around the 'religious slot' in the morning. We decided to run from 10.30 to midday once a month on a Thursday morning, starting off with some sort of story telling, followed by a related activity, then social and play time with some circle singing at the end to round it off. The story telling drew initially upon some resources recommended to me by the Diocesan Children's Officer, including techniques of presentation and suggestions for activities. I have to admit to be not being at ease with this and really wondering whether going along with such immediately accessible themes as Easter was really the best way to approach the sessions. Trying to get toddlers 'involved' in the way that worked much more easily with older children at school or in family services was an uphill task. Even working out how to get and retain their attention for anything other than a couple of minutes created problems. I really needed more understanding of child development and what one could reasonably expect to be able to do with this age group. Having a professional on the committee who had set up and run nursery provision was a huge advantage as I struggled with this unfamiliar territory.

However, it did raise in a very acute form the question of how one was to interpret, let alone communicate the content of the Christian tradition to anybody who was unfamiliar with it, and that included some of the mothers let alone the toddlers. What was the objective here and what should we sensibly be aiming to achieve? Was it just a matter of conveying a general moral point wrapped up in the stories of a particular historical tradition? For instance, getting across to this age group a point about sharing with others was quite a challenge in itself, without having to explain details about the New Testament context which would make sense of the specific story. I did reach the conclusion after a while that what we were doing was offering the parents as much as the children an encounter with the stories of the tradition, given that some of them did not themselves have a church background and therefore lacked the 'discourse' that others of us had grown up with. There were discussions amongst the mothers about buying Bible story books for their children that they could use at home, which I took as a positive sign.

On a broader level it led me to ask to what extent the Christian identity – whatever was meant by that – depended upon the regular encounter with Bible stories which had been the staple diet of Sunday schools and church activities for earlier generations. It seemed to me that this regular encounter was indeed significant, not because at an early age one would understand or know what to make of the stories, but simply because they form one of the main structures of passing on the tradition. If you do not know the stories because you have not grown up within that setting then you are not formed as a person from within that tradition and your stories will come from elsewhere.

After the first six months our numbers had grown with 12 to 15 families attending. This exceeded our original expectations and showed that we were obviously meeting a need within the area. By this stage it was also becoming clear that the local playgroup would not survive much longer. Given that this would mean that we were the only pre-school provision left in the parishes it seemed reasonable to invest more time into the project. The suggestion had already been made that we increase the frequency of meetings and so the committee decided that we would do this from the New Year onwards. This was a 'step-change' for us as a committee and required much greater organization and agreement about our objectives and structure. I will return to other aspects of this shortly. In terms of content though we decided that one session should continue to be centered on the 'vicar's slot', geared potentially to the monthly family service the following Sunday, and that the other session would be run more as play and activity and be organized by the committee but with myself present for continuity and support. We also agreed that I would tackle some of the famous stories from the Old Testament during the year in addition to obvious themes from the church's calendar. Now this was a real challenge because the really 'good' stories from the Old Testament are liberally strewn with sex and violence! What about the story of David and Goliath and the uncensored versions of David's later life, let alone Samson and Delilah? If we were going to use these resources did we need to 'water them down' or else just tell them in full gory details because that is what is there? We decided there was no point watering them down but that they should be told as they are, otherwise why use those stories at all? Just how much of the story would be absorbed by the children it is always difficult to assess. However, we concluded that this was also of benefit for some of the parents, particularly those who were unfamiliar with the Christian tradition.

In a way it has taken us back to a very 'simple' and old-fashioned sounding method of communicating the faith. Just tell the stories and thus embed them in people's psyche because without that they cannot be formed by or grow up within a specifically Christian context. If they do not encounter these stories they will most certainly encounter others from within the surrounding culture and grow up within the 'discourses' which underlie that context. Those of us who had been brought up within the church had grown up with the stories and the pictures associated with them and, despite the sex and violence, had hopefully not been harmed by them. In any case, are they really any more extreme than the stories watched on TV soaps and cartoons daily by our children? However, although I can see the force of this in practical terms and, in our second year of operating on a twice-monthly basis we are going to cover some of the best-known New Testament stories, I still wonder exactly what it is that is being communicated to both children and parents and what it is that we should be aiming to achieve? Will any old content do just so long as it is to be found within the Bible? Would any other stories do just as well or even better, provided that they illustrated the ideas or values that lie behind the story? How do we help people of all ages to make connections between these distant accounts and life as they now encounter it and what then gets lost in the translation? For the moment I would say that these remain open questions for our particular group but that it has been encouraging that people do not appear to stay away from it because we use explicit Christian content. The fact that we do lots of other things besides I am sure is crucial, but then this is perhaps the best way of offering those outside the tradition a genuine but non-threatening encounter with the tradition. Given that this is work in progress we continue to learn from and reflect upon our current practice.

Encountering the Establishment

One of my major concerns having created this new group was how it would relate to the existing and well-established church constituency. The particular church to which this group would be attached, the parish in which the hall is set and the church where the monthly family service is held, has a very strong social element based on a number of families whose own children had grown up together. These children have now moved on through university and out into the world of work and the population structure is such that they are not being replaced by the next generation. So the regular congregation of this church is static, tight-knit, but also welcoming and efficient and eager to encourage younger families into their number. There are interesting issues here about the evolution or life-cycle of congregations in small communities and the constant question of how to secure the succession and bring new and younger people into the orbit of such churches. There is also the issue of different cultures and expectations and I could see this possibly being another barrier to integration. In many ways I did not want the new grouping to 'integrate' in a seamless fashion and for the existing congregation to continue as if nothing had changed, rather I saw them as being the 'other' who might question and challenge in creative ways. This might be the one way in which the establishment could be forced to look afresh at itself and be required to respond to a different set of questions. Hence what happened as the Toddler group became itself more established would be a test of the existing social grouping.

Following the pattern of many other such projects we invited the church congregation to send some adult helpers to each of the Toddler sessions. We heard of stories where friendly 'grannies' who attended on a regular basis formed a sort of anchor for the younger mothers and also a sounding board when they needed to share problems and questions. They could also assist in practical ways by making drinks and setting-up and clearing away afterwards. This invitation to help was welcomed by some of the ladies in the congregation and a rota of adult helpers was established. As with any new project there were times when this did not always run smoothly and some of the adult helpers questioned what their role really was and were left standing around without any clear objective. What emerged fairly quickly was that two of the 'older' ladies were very committed to the project and were prepared to be present for most of the sessions which offered continuity and better pastoral contact. One of these has subsequently come onto the organizing committee in order to further cement this contact. Her husband has also been very supportive in setting up the room beforehand and in other important practical ways. Over the months this has led to a deepening of relationships between the different generations and eased the passage of the younger families into other church activities. I strongly believe that this is one of the most significant factors in any process of growth and development. The establishment of relationships of trust and confidence with key 'others' is fundamental to any project that supports personal change. Such relationships take time and continuity in order to develop and cannot simply be wished into existence by good intentions. This is one of the cornerstones of parochial ministry and one that is often neglected. The investment of time, including staying with the various settings and groups through the early stages of feeling awkward and superfluous to requirements, is essential if further work is to develop. The fruits of others' willingness to befriend and give time to Toddlers has begun to show in the relationships that have now developed.

Another aspect of this was clearly going to be the linkage of the Toddlers session to the existing family service. In the first year of the project when we were still only operating once a month there was only intermittent contact with a particular family occasionally attending the church service. However, once we decided to meet twice a month it raised the question of a stronger link between the two 'services'. One of my committee members sensibly suggested that the vicar's slot should be in the session immediately preceding the family service so that work by the Toddlers could be used and displayed for the benefit of the wider congregation. Although the principle is correct time commitments of the parents involved has meant that this has worked better on some occasions than on others. When it has worked it has made a positive impact on the rest of the congregation who are generally delighted to see that new young families are now becoming part of church life and like to see the sort of activities that they themselves remember from earlier days. It is the familiar point that working with children generally wins 'brownie points' whatever it is you actually do.

From the beginning of 2003 the Toddlers have made a growing impact upon our regular church worship. Christmas 2003 was an excellent example of this where the Toddlers performed a simple Christmas activity at the local school and at the Christmas Eve children's service and where Toddlers' families appeared in numbers at all of the church services including taking part in the choir at the carol service. A new constituency has come into existence and this is becoming evident to the existing church congregations to the point where their views and needs have to be taken into account. In that sense my idea that they would be the 'other' breaking open the existing structures and relationships has proved well founded. It has also meant that some of the young families have formed their own social grouping outside Toddlers and created a sub-community with its own distinctive culture, although others are conscious of the dangers of forming cliques and are careful to avoid this possibility. How quickly this becomes its own new 'establishment' which others cannot break into is an interesting question. My hope is that this group's identity and sense of itself will remain open enough to enable others to join and benefit from it. Again I believe this is a critical issue for all church activities. Is this simply another 'enclave of interim intimacy' that will last as long as certain people remain committed to it and gain from it, or will it be both open and sustainable in the longer term? At this early stage we cannot know the answers to this.

This is not to say that relationships between the new and the not-so-new have always been smooth and without their points of tension. The young mothers have encountered resistance to the presence of Toddlers in the village hall and the vexed question of storage space has been a difficult one to resolve. The hall committee is another 'establishment' of its own, with its own particularly important people and relationships. It took a period of 'negotiation' for Toddlers to get agreement to have their own storage cupboard and, even now, they could always use more space than is strictly allowed. Putting pictures up around the wall and getting a display board in church are further objectives that have yet to be achieved! However, the processes of building up new relationships are now well underway and there is no question that this new group is having an impact upon the wider church community. What is not yet clear is whether this is a matter of integrating the new into the existing group or whether a different culture is being created.

Issues of lifestyle

One of the unknown questions when we started the group was that of how many mothers would be around on a regular basis, let alone prepared to commit them-selves to a monthly meeting. Given that a considerable number of our potential constituents lived on the new estate these are families with both parents working, even though the women might only be working part-time. The impact of the pressures of globalization was bound to play a part in what was possible. Houses on the estate (this is at the end of 2003) are in the region of £250,000 thus requiring a considerable financial outlay in terms of a mortgage and of course all the other trappings of the lifestyle which is often a part of living in such locations. For many couples this requires that both partners contribute and there is a sense of existing with the constant threat of redundancy or possible re-location. The affluence that is clearly there on the surface obscures the pressures that lurk not far below. This combined with what both Trade Unions and government sources now tell us is an unfavourable work-life balance in this country all contribute to the fear that it is not going to be possible to create any locally-based sustainable community activity. Or it could be that it is exactly these pressures which make such community activity that much more important and attractive as an antidote to the work-driven lifestyle.

It is difficult to talk about individual circumstances although such projects always depend upon these, but some features do need to be mentioned. Of the three mothers on the committee two work part-time but one is not working. As it is this mother who has the professional skills that have been so crucial in creating a successful group we would have to say that we have been remarkably fortunate in having the benefit of her time and gifts. Once she returns to work it is her intention to remain committed to the group, although one always hopes that others might also have come forward by then. Of the other mothers who are now regulars about half are working part-time. The interesting and encouraging point is that although we have lost some who have gone back to work or who are not in control of their working hours, a number have contrived to keep Thursday free just so that they can bring their children to Toddlers. Others have also steered away from sending their children to nursery on a Thursday for the same reason. I assume that this shows that we are meeting a need of some sort and that the quality of what we have created is such that mothers are willing to design their individual timetables around the group meetings. This also means that a number of them are free to meet together outside Toddlers on the intervening weeks thus creating further social life and mutual support. The level of commitment to the group is high, so much so that we had a full turn out despite problems of snow and ice making driving the lanes dangerous and reservations from the 'grannies' about running the session at all. The pressure is on us as organizers to keep the doors open and not allow too many gaps in the programme even during the summer.

Is this because the need for mutual support and contact is that much greater given work pressures and lifestyle? I think that may well be the case. Although some of the mothers have their own mothers living reasonably close and some of them also come to Toddlers from time to time, for others there is the problem of isolation from family support. This section of one's life brings its own difficulties regardless of the external economic factors, and to be able to go somewhere comfortable and relaxed where there are other young mothers around, and to know that one is not alone in the problems faced is of considerable value. That the local church happens to provide such an occasion is largely co-incidental on one level, but is a potential opportunity to show that the church can offer something useful on another. It has been encouraging that all the mothers with new babies brought them for baptism in one or other of my four churches and even adopted a similar approach to the liturgy having seen this in operation at each other's services. This included using some of the Toddlers songs, hymns and musical instruments as part of the baptism service. Although some of these families have a church background, others do not, but have gained confidence in handling the unfamiliar context through the personal relationships that have developed.

The pressure on husbands is perhaps the hidden factor in all of this. I know of one family where the father works in London. This means he has to leave the house before 6 every morning and does not return until after 7 in the evening. One of the mothers leaves for work at 7.30 a.m. often not returning until 7.30 at night. This leaves precious little time for family life and means that weekends are subject to increased expectations. Everything else that needs to happen outside work has to happen at weekends. This places possible church attendance a long way down the list of priorities. It also means that little or no time is available for community or social activity during weekday evenings. This is a national problem creating difficulties for most voluntary groups of which the church is simply one. Hence the inability to create sustainable community activity in growing numbers of places and the moves by some churches to shift the focus of worship and social life away from weekends altogether. However, I also wonder how sustainable this lifestyle is in itself. Perhaps one can live with it for a certain length of time or up until a certain age, but it must take its toll on both energy and relationships. In one way I could argue that Toddlers is helping to sustain families in the midst of such pressures but in another I would hope that these families will start asking themselves the question of whether this is really worth it. My instinct is that, if people were to take the risk of stopping to think about this, they might well decide that the costs are too high. But then, what is the alternative? It may be easier simply to struggle on and enjoy the fruits of one's labours through the products of conspicuous consumption – high performance cars, foreign holidays, regular updates of domestic goods etc – than to stand back and question what this is all about. Will there come a point where people begin to feel trapped by this? As the costs of education, health care and housing continue to rise the prospects for many can only be 'more of the same' but with ever greater risks and demands. In the midst of this Toddlers, school, church and community play a holding operation, creating their enclaves of interim intimacy for those who are living much closer to the edge than they are prepared to admit.

Toddlers and the wider community

I had known from the start that setting up our own church group could prove divisive and continued to be concerned about this as Toddlers became more established. It was somewhat difficult to visit what was left of the existing playgroup each Friday knowing that our numbers and resources were growing. However, I think that events have shown that this was the correct course of action and that it is vital that we retain some pre-school provision within the parishes. The particular mothers who were involved in the playgroup have also now moved on in terms of their own lives and are participating in the lives of their children's schools rather than catering for the younger age group. In any case, one of our objectives is to foster links with the local school and to be a possible feeder to them, which matches one of the aims of the original playgroup. Toddlers is enabling us to keep families rooted in the community even though some of the children will also go to nurseries elsewhere.

Our links with the local school are developing satisfactorily. From time to time a teacher will visit one of our sessions and we have been invited back into school for certain events. Some of the mothers who are bringing their second child to Toddlers already have an elder child at the school, so that makes the connections that much more solid. I have now drafted two parents from Toddler's families onto the school governors as we move to bring in new blood and fresh skills so it is perfectly natural to pursue ad hoc conversations about school matters during Toddlers sessions. A major issue for the school is that we do not have any before or after school provision, nor do we have a nursery in the parishes and we know that we lose some children to other schools simply because we do not offer those facilities. Having followed up some potential leads on this front what we have been able to do is to improve our existing accommodation by building a new classroom. This has meant a considerable financial commitment from the governors as, because it is a Voluntary Aided school, the governors are responsible for raising 10% of any capital costs. We are in the process of reaching our £15,000 target towards the cost of new building works which includes other items in addition to the new classroom. However, this is not the limit of our ambitions.

Our longer term aim is to have our own nursery provision on site. Whether it is run privately is not an issue for us, but we do need to offer this facility. Toddlers is important here because it is, in some ways, a holding operation and an interim measure to keep the interest and attention of potential parents in the hope that we will, in due course, be able to provide nursery education as well. The village hall in this part of the parishes is in need of rebuilding and has made a number of applications to the National Lottery for funds, so far without success. It is the hall which the playgroup did use and which new parents were increasingly unhappy with because of its deteriorating physical state. It is located on the other side of a busy main road from the school, which is a major problem for any potential shared usage. A number of us have been arguing for some time that the hall should consider moving next door to the school, probably onto what is now the school playing field. This would create a campus, relieve traffic problems and enable the hall committee to access greater funding for their project because this would be a shared usage facility with the school. After many months of no real progress, the hall committee have decided to pursue these conversations with the school governors. I personally think that this could be the most significant development for both school and community since the building of the new estate. However, this would not be a straightforward project and would demand a considerable investment of time and energy from both sides. If this were to come about then all of our children's work could be based on the same site, within walking distance for the families on the new estate, and perhaps Toddlers would no longer be needed. In the meantime however we continue to thrive and to bridge the gap in pre-school provision. In that sense our role within the wider community is also of significance and any possible bad feeling that may have arisen has to be handled for the cause of a greater good.

Another aspect of this is undoubtedly the differences in lifestyle and disposable income between the 'locals' who were prime movers in the playgroup and the 'newcomers' who have become the constituency for Toddlers. This is reflected in the higher expectations that the latter group possess when it comes to the provision of children's facilities. The hall which nobody before had thought a problem is suddenly seen as a poor and inadequate facility. The levels of activity and the standards of care at the playgroup were also sometimes criticized by mothers who had experienced better in other places. The lack of organization behind the running of the playgroup was a long running problem. Their finances were never quite in order and money always seemed to be running short. In addition to this the resistance to go for OFSTED registration all combined to give a picture of a group that was behind the time and refusing to change. Toddlers has therefore been under pressure not to fall into this trap, although OFSTED registration is not an issue for us because this is still a mothers and toddlers group where a parent or carer stays on site and takes responsibility for the child. Yet these differences in expectations have been a significant source of tension and I have had to make my stand with the newcomers simply because this is the general direction of things in this field and if one does not keep up to speed with current developments one must expect not to survive. This is a hard lesson to learn and, sadly, does appear to devalue the hard work and commitment of those who ran the earlier facility. As already noted though, it is a fact of life that all community activity now requires a higher degree of organization and professionalism and that even churches need volunteers who can offer the appropriate skills in order to cope in this environment. That is not so much of a problem in this particular locality, but in others it will be a major issue. The church is being swallowed up by this aspect of contemporary culture, appropriated or 'eaten' and it is hard to resist being pulled across this particular boundary.

Toddlers as a learning organization

The drive towards professional standards can also be seen as a positive opportunity for the individuals involved to further their own personal and professional development. Thus I want to now describe some of the decisions we have taken and activities that have been organized in order to argue the case that, although we are a small-scale voluntary group, we are also a 'learning organization'. We learnt from the experience of the playgroup that we needed to get our house in order from the very start and to have appropriate structures and documents in place. The pressure for this became greater once we made the decision to offer two sessions a month rather than one. The difference in scale between the two patterns was itself an eye-opener for the committee. Up until that point we had held the odd ad hoc meeting with myself and three of the key mothers in order to construct a programme and some activities and to agree on the purchasing of resources. However, doubling the number of sessions required more than a doubling of our level of organization.

First we decided that we needed a constitution. It did not need to be anything too complicated but it meant that we would have a document to fall back on should there ever be any disputes or challenges to what we were doing or should we want to apply for external funding. It was fortunate that we were able to set up with monies from other local sources and to avoid any initial fundraising. I have no doubt that the churches themselves would have supported this initiative had we needed to ask. The constitution gives us an identity and some clear parameters. So our aim is 'to provide a monthly service and a monthly social meeting for pre-school age children with a parent or carer for those within the Four Square parishes'. This enables us to limit access to the group although it also allows us some flexibility when that is thought appropriate. There is no way in which we could service a completely open group where parents just came from anywhere in the area because we happen to provide a good facility. This would swamp the existing group and detract from the church basis of it. Our objectives then follow on from that aim and include providing a brief act of worship introducing themes from the Christian tradition; offering parents and carers an opportunity to meet and support one another; providing the space for creative play in a safe environment; working within Diocesan child protection guidelines and fostering links with other local groups including the school and the family service. We then have a formal committee structure with chair, treasurer and secretary and they are accountable to the Four Square parishes through the vicar. We have our own bank account, although we share with the Sunday school and proper accounts are kept and produced by our treasurer. Unlike many other groups we do make a small charge per session. This was originally £1.50 for a first child and less for a subsequent one, but we have raised this to £2.00 and nobody has objected. We have regular overheads such as rent for the hall and money for the meter as well as drinks and biscuits so we aim to cover those costs through our charging policy. Other resources have been bought out of existing funds, although the committee's own fund-raising efforts have meant that we have more than replaced whatever we spent out of the original account. Fund raising so far has been by taking stalls to other events and by committee members taking part in a sponsored walk, money from which was shared with a national charity and a local beneficiary of the participants' choice. Committee members have shown considerable commitment and initiative and also enjoyed taking part in these activities. This is a major way in which Toddlers has led to other things and been part of the development of the individuals involved.

We have also sponsored a parent from outside the immediate parishes who took part in the London marathon in order to raise money for a particular children's charity and run a St John Ambulance training day for parents and grandparents on how to deal with young children in an emergency, as a result of which each participant received a certificate. These are small scale in themselves but important spin-offs from the core activity that, hopefully, display a wider concern and awareness of the needs of others. That is what I would want and expect from any church-based group, but it has to happen because others believe it is appropriate, not because the vicar wants it to.

In what other ways could we be said to be a *learning organization*? I believe that the whole process by which we have reached where we are now has been one of personal and group development – as one would expect of any community activity. The challenge of moving from once a month to twice a month really was a test of our capacity to cope with change. For at least the first 6 months of this new pattern we were constantly reviewing and revising what we did. Achieving a balance and a difference between the vicar's session and the social session was a major challenge. In the early months it was difficult to tell the difference between the two in terms of either structure or content. We struggled with this as a committee and held a number of formal and informal meetings to try to work out the best way of doing this. It now feels as though we have settled into a pattern that is so familiar and comfortable that it is hard to imagine we ever had these problems, but it was not that way until relatively recently. There were tensions between the members of the committee over who did what and when and concern that too much was falling on the shoulders of our 'professional' simply because she is so good at the activities. This is common to most voluntary groups with other people always being happy to stand back and let somebody else with the skills and time deal with the bulk of the work. I would not say that this tension has been fully resolved and there may yet be the need to bring others onto the committee in due course in order to share the workload a little more evenly. However, this is the raw material of our learning about ourselves and of how to work with other people. Resolving differences is no small skill whatever the context. At the moment we appear to have evolved a structure for each session that 'works' but I think that part of that is also that those who attend now implicitly understand what will happen when and why so it does not require explanation. I presume that such community groups develop their own culture over time and that makes the levels of decision-making less controversial.

Perhaps the prime example of this was our handling of Christmas. For our first Christmas together, remembering that we were still only holding one session per month at that stage, we tried to do too much in one morning. It was complicated by the fact that we had advertised this as an open session with Father Christmas visiting so we had families who did not otherwise attend and children who were extra-excited and disruptive. Father Christmas was unavoidably delayed in his arrival, which did not help matters, and it was generally a morning that was constantly running out of control to the point where many of the regulars, both children and parents did not enjoy the experience. It was a nightmare to be honest and the committee realized that we had got this badly wrong. Clearly we had to learn from this for our second time around. We started thinking about this before the summer and decided to run our two sessions on consecutive weeks before Christmas, one as a 'service' slot with preparation for our Christmas 'play' to be performed at school and at the Christmas Eve service and the second as a party for the children. We actually performed our short play on both sessions but this was all to the good. This year there was no Father Christmas, instead the vicar got to hand out the presents! Of course organizing presents when one never quite knows who is going to be there and who not is itself a problem. However, all went much more smoothly and, this time, we all enjoyed it rather than wishing Christmas would be over as quickly as possible. There is talk next Christmas of bringing Father Christmas back again, but this is something we will need to discuss and review.

All of this is hardly of any great importance in one way, but it is the raw material of our learning in another and thus not to be underestimated. The committee members are bound to reflect upon what happens and to constantly refine and re-order our activities and structures accordingly. Things will also need to change as the children who are now regulars either leave to move on to school, or progress from babies to toddlers and thus require different levels of activity. The whole feel of such a group can alter during the course of a few months as suddenly the fairly static infants start crawling and then walking. The group itself is forced to re-think on a regular basis as what worked a short time ago is no longer appropriate now. If we are not a learning organization, capable of looking at ourselves and realizing that we have to adapt and change we will not be able to deliver our objectives and provide the quality of service that others demand. Nothing stands still for very long when you are working with young children!

Blurred encounters

In conclusion I want to draw out a number of areas where previously secure boundaries are being crossed and identities are perhaps becoming blurred. As stated previously, I do not necessarily see this as a problem but more a reflection on where things are more generally. Without a willingness to risk being appropriated it seems unlikely that anything significant would have happened, certainly in the case of our local children's work.

The way in which we use explicit Christian content in the context of what otherwise might appear to be a secular mothers and toddlers group is a clear example of this. I often wonder how effective our communication of the Christian tradition actually is, but then one would probably be asking that same question of anything one was doing with this age group. The fact that mothers tell me afterwards that the children have been asking questions about God or some other related topic I take as a sign that something at least is getting through. In the Lent course of 2004 we offered parents a chance to talk about exactly those sorts of questions and how we might then respond to them. I still believe that this is also about what the unchurched adults pick up about the tradition along the way and even more about them feeling comfortable with the people who form the local congregation and recognizing that the church can offer something that is of practical benefit. In that sense the specific content is not itself so important. However, I do also believe that it is easy for those of us who have been brought up in the tradition to underplay the importance of regular encounters with the stories that carry that tradition and that of simply being around in the general atmosphere. So some sort of balance between content and appropriate structure is still important. To abandon any reference to the Christian faith would be to betray our chosen identity. Having said that, to overplay our hand and present material that was too heavy or inaccessible, would also be a mistake. Others might achieve the balance in a different way but we feel that what we do is appropriate for our context.

The question of how, if at all, this activity will translate into more structured forms of churchgoing and support, is a very interesting one. Much has been written recently about 'liquid church', adopting Bauman's contrast between solid and liquid that is illuminating in other spheres of social life (Bauman 2000). One could easily argue that Toddlers is a good example of liquid church. It does not meet in the church; it meets during the week not on Sunday; it includes certain elements that are not directly related to the Christian tradition and thus encompasses non-church-goers; above all it may not feed directly into regular patterns of church attendance or belonging. Although some of our members are from a church background and attend family services and other events, many do not come to anything outside Toddlers itself. So if the church as institution is a solid requiring commitment to its structures and the capacity to reproduce itself by bringing in new members, the Toddlers is liquid in that it may not have a direct pay-off for the local church. It may also be a 'for-the-time-being-only' group, one that exists for as long as its current members have a use for it but will cease as their children move on to school and its related social life. While all of this is perfectly acceptable there is still the question, for some of us at least, as to how the church as institution will survive in the longer term if it is not possible to convert some of the liquid into a more solid commitment. We are crossing a boundary into a social pattern that itself undermines the sustainability of community and voluntary activity. Or is it that this is now the form that such activity will have to take given other changing social structures and attitudes. Are we all condemned to become interim enclaves surviving only for as long as we perform a practical role and provide a 'quality service'? However, if all becomes liquid will there be enough institution left for the Christian tradition to be able to reproduce itself over time? I do not think we can yet know the answers to such questions, but there is no doubt that Toddlers is another example of solid church crossing the boundary into liquid church.

I think it should be clear by now that another cultural boundary that is under threat is that between voluntary and professional. We have seen this in the growing expectations of parents of the standards they require of all childcare activities, even those that are voluntary. There is no doubt that we are under pressure to deliver a high quality of content, structure and activity and that the committee has to handle the running of the group in a professional manner. If we begin to fail in this mothers will vote with their feet and take their children elsewhere. It is all very well having a local group to attend where one can meet one's friends and be part of the local community, but that, in itself, will not be enough to hold their commitment unless we continue to 'deliver the goods'. Schools, churches and all locally based groups are now subject to consumer choice. This is simply the way that most people make their decisions these days. Part of me objects strongly to this and wants to see a genuine commitment to the locality and its facilities, come what may, but this is unrealistic. We operate in a competitive environment where we have to deliver in order to survive. It is the same for schools and probably for all institutions because there is no longer any local monopoly of service provision. One could argue that this is to have crossed the boundary into the culture of consumer choice which brings its own dangers of elitism and rationing according to income. However, once again, it is where we are now and, if local church is to create locations for encounter and stand a chance of doing this type of community work it has to play by these rules, at least for the time being. Perhaps opportunities for an alternative approach can be presented through a concern for charitable activity, but I think these are limited and we have to accept that the voluntary sector generally now demands much higher degrees of professionalism if it is to attract both volunteers and potential 'clients'.

This seems to me to link quite strongly with the ideas of Castells and Beck as described in the previous chapter. What is operating now is a tension between a sense of self that is still based on locality and community and the sense of self that is determined by the forces of the global economy. The latter works on the principles of consumer choice and the acceptance that there are no subsidies for projects that cannot deliver quality at the right price, whereas those engaged in family and community life still imagine they are operating on the basis of whatever a particular locality happens to provide, whatever its quality or cost. There is a self that is universal, participating as a working person in that competitive environment and a self that claims to be geared to other 'softer' values and will support local activity come what may. However, the risks involved in pursuing the latter path and getting things badly wrong – e.g. by choosing an inadequate local school for one's child – are now so serious in terms of future life and work opportunities, that very few are likely to sacrifice choice in favour of local commitment. The universal wins out over the local, then leaving an uneasy conscience and the fear that one might one day need the local after all and that it might no longer be there if all support has disappeared. This boundary is blurred and there are no easy ways of resolving such tensions so the local does carry on, sometimes with exaggerated enthusiasm in order to compensate for the real threats and dangers. Local church and all related activities are stuck firmly in the middle of this, forced to face in both directions at once. It is where we all are at the moment.

A further boundary is that between locals and newcomers, an almost constant feature of 'rural' life. Toddlers certainly straddled this one and probably came down on the side of the newcomers for some of the reasons just expressed above. Yet there is also a boundary between the existing local church establishment and new people perhaps needing to find ways into a locality and part of my role is to provide those locations for encounter which may ease that process. Then the new constituency may well become an establishment of its own and itself need the challenge of the 'other' in order to keep it open and reflective. Blurring the boundaries or trying to keep them fluid is an essential part of this task. Using Derrida's language it is about deconstruction, releasing the other that is always present in any situation in order to prevent the stabilization that turns into exclusivism and forms of fundamentalism. A bit of regular instability is a good antidote to the hardening of the boundaries!

The final area worthy of note returns us to the central issue of identity. The changing role of women, the subsequent destabilization of family life and confusion for men in their roles, both of these exacerbated by rapid economic and social change, are background features of much children's work. These somewhat threatening realities are often kept beneath the surface just because nobody is comfortable with handling them or admitting that they might have a problem here. Thus the façade of respectability and success measured by the external symbols of house, cars, holidays and other domestic accessories has to hold firm if the tidal waves of uncertainty are to be held back. Sometimes the pressures begin to show, but they are likely to be kept behind closed doors for fear of public failure in the challenge of being in charge of one's life. I often feel that there is a contest going on amongst the younger families and I would want to say that there is then a danger that the real issues are being neglected. However, this is a boundary of personal development that individuals must now cross for themselves as and when and if they are ready. In the meantime we construct our sense of identity by using the products of our culture and manipulating the symbols of economic success. I would like to think that the Christian tradition offers an alternative to this and that this might be communicated despite the culture in which we operate. If we are failing in this then perhaps we have been appropriated and no longer offer glimpses of an open identity.

I want to look more deeply into this in the next chapter but I will close by saying that Toddlers has been effective in responding to the level of operation that I term pre-autonomous, that of feelings and of the subjective generally, often picking up and reacting sympathetically to personal problems and the need for pastoral support that surface where there is trust and confidence in one another. Whether we have been quite so effective at the further level of self-conscious and reflective personal development and with the sort of issues facing the committee is not quite so clear – let us call this autonomy for the sake of argument. Then there is a further level that lurks beneath those more difficult questions of identity, unknown areas of human development highlighted by some feminists and other philosophers, that which I might refer to as the messianic glimpse of what it is we might become. Here we are moving into uncharted territory, the open or project identity. Perhaps Toddlers has not yet taken these steps into the unknown.

6

Down on the farm

Introduction

The accounts offered in this chapter relate to local experiences during the Foot and Mouth outbreak of 2001. However, before moving on to these I want to make it clear how and why they fit into the wider argument. At the close of the previous chapter I raised the question of whether Toddlers had taken our thinking beyond the pre-autonomous level or simply concentrated activities around the dimension of feelings and immediate pastoral responses. Although I introduced a number of other themes into the discussion linking our project to wider concerns about the impact of globalization on family and community life it would be inaccurate to suggest that these were in any way explicit. They are background concerns that are acknowledged only fleetingly and indirectly through individual encounters rather than being formally or structurally recognized at a collective level. There is also the danger of creating just another establishment or enclosed constituency which, in its turn, fails to respond to others who do not immediately fit its social pattern. Is this another enclave of interim intimacy or could it be the springboard for the evolution of a more open identity? Under what conditions would such a transformation be more likely to happen? As suggested, it is perhaps too early to offer definitive answers to these questions, but the fear is there that the personal development of the individuals involved will get stuck at the stage which represents the limit of their own comfort zone. There are questions which they would rather not ask and uncertainties that they would rather not face.

Why is this a problem and why is it important for our subject of relating the Christian tradition to the surrounding culture? An obvious answer is that it restricts and limits the scope of church activity to the private, the personal and the domestic. Now there is the wider point acknowledged by virtue of feminist debate that these are themselves part of the broader political discussions. The domestic agenda is indeed also a political one and what happens to women and families in schooling and childcare domains is a legitimate and neglected matter for public debate. However, this is not quite the same when it comes to handling the Christian tradition. What

93

we have seen in the Children's Festival and Toddlers projects are classic church-based pastoral support activities which tend not to impact upon discussions of the wider political context let alone concerns about globalization. The local church through its community based action provides individual pastoral support that may indeed assist particular families in surviving the pressures created by greater job insecurity and social mobility but in no way encourages people to think more deeply about their lives or to question why they choose to live under these pressures. It could thus be deemed to be collusive rather than critical and may be open to the objection that it has been swallowed up or eaten by the very social values that it might be expected to critique. Has the local church's desperation to establish a role for itself led it, once again, across the boundary into alien territory where its own approach to matters of family and culture has been irrevocably compromised? I would of course argue that this is not the case, but then I would have to be able to show how this activity might still foster a more critical engagement with the cultural values. This is why I need to develop further the ideas of pre-autonomy and post-autonomy that will emerge later in this chapter.

It can be seen however that this is simply a local manifestation of a wider debate for church involvement. As long as Christianity is identified with the 'others' of reason, the realm of the subjective, personal, private and domestic, it cannot gain a foothold in the public debates about politics, economics and social structures. It remains restricted and constrained by where it is seen to fit into people's lives and by its own comfort zone. Christians are more at ease with the 'soft values' related to the sphere of relationships than with the 'hard values' which determine economic and political life. Even when we gain a voice in public life it is invariably on those terms and with the understanding that we somehow represent a more 'caring' side to whatever public activity is involved. The churches generally are not very good at issues of business and organization let alone at making the tough decisions that are called for in the 'real' world. Unfortunately our own internal practice on matters of finance and personnel invariably bears this out, even though it is individuals and their pastoral care that suffers in the process. Frankly I much prefer to attend meetings of the Festival Housing Group than most church gatherings for the simple reason that decisions do get made after open discussion and life moves on, whereas church meetings tend to talk for ever, try to please everybody and end up leading to inaction and frustration.

However, if this too is to change it requires a broader underlying approach to human subjectivity, one which challenges the demarcation line between the autonomy which supposedly determines the business world and the pre-autonomy which is characteristic of the church-based culture. What I intend to show now is that an over-emphasis upon autonomy as encountered in the political responses to the Foot and Mouth outbreak is as inadequate as the tendencies in church activity to concentrate upon the pre-autonomous level of human operation. The requirement to work towards an open or project identity demands a further dimension of human subjectivity for which we will need to draw upon other external resources as well as some from the Christian tradition. Only in this way will the Christian tradition develop a firmer basis for engagement with public life.

The outbreak of Foot and Mouth

Although this particular outbreak only affected certain parts of the country and most urban areas were of course untouched, the impact of these events upon those directly involved was significant both economically and emotionally. It began officially in the early months of 2001 with a diagnosed case in the North East of England. Since the previous outbreak had been in 1967 there were not so many people around who had any experience of what this might mean. Was this going to be a national crisis, one that put our rural areas into effective quarantine and brought large areas of the countryside to a standstill thus damaging other economic activity? Was this the final nail in the coffin of British agriculture adding insult to the injury of BSE and the declining incomes of many farms? This is very much what it felt like at the time and I think there is no doubt that the events of 2001 have hastened the demise of parts of the farming industry.

The worst affected areas were Cumbria, Wales and Devon, each still heavily dependent upon farming and the related tourist industry. However, this part of Worcestershire was also drawn into the spider's web of disease through the movement of farm animals across the country. We were forced to close one of my four churches for a period of time because it was adjacent to a farm and very close to a supposedly infected area. A number of farmers and their families were confined to their properties for some weeks leaving telephone calls as the only means of contact. I wrote my own list of the farmers in the parishes and made a point of phoning round them during the crisis in order to maintain at least limited contact. There was considerable uncertainty as to what was happening or how long this would last and indeed over what action should be taken at a local level. The story was one of confusion and also of suspicion towards central government who, it was suggested, either did not know what they were doing or were deliberately aggravating the outbreak in order to further decimate certain aspects of farming in this country. What I encountered as a locally-based parish priest were the perceptions and deeply held feelings which surfaced as the outbreak took a hold and the almost complete failure of the official authorities to acknowledge let alone address that pastoral dimension of what was happening. Hence it is those stories and their implications for my general argument that I will now focus on.

As the accounts of what was happening began to appear in the press it was clear that one complete dimension of events was being ignored by the then government agency MAFF. The proposed solution to limit the scope of the outbreak was to cull not just the infected animals but all those on properties that were contiguous with the infected farms. This rapidly became a matter of considerable controversy with farmers themselves objecting that the appropriate response would be a mass vaccination of stock instead. As an outsider and a non-expert on the scientific aspects of this I found it very difficult to grasp and assess the arguments. There were local discrepancies as to the definition of contiguous which did nothing to help the psychological state of the farmers who were in the middle of all this. It seemed as though the government were determined to implement this strategy and would only listen to the advice of their own particular scientific 'experts' who were telling them what they wanted or expected to hear. Inevitably the argument polarized into a debate between the objectivity and rationality of these particular scientific experts as presented in this way by the government and the subjective and emotional responses of a minority of environmentally inclined onlookers who were unaware of the commercial nature of contemporary farming. Vaccination was presented as the 'soft' but ineffective option that would do more harm than good to the farming industry as potential importers of British meat would fear that the disease was still in the stock. Any farmers who went public with their objections to this strategy were portrayed as eccentric and unrepresentative and not fully aware of the scientific and political arguments. Alternative web sites started to appear giving the 'real story' behind what was going on and suggesting that the government's motives for going down this route were less than honourable. It was suggested that they had already done a deal with other EU partners to destroy much of the UK's sheep population and this was their perfect pretence or cover for taking this action.

I began to ask questions about what was really happening in all this and came up with a number of related answers. There is no doubt that there was animosity and suspicion between the farming community and the New Labour government based not only on political differences but also on a perceived lack of sympathy and understanding for the 'rural way of life' amongst government leaders. The idea that the latter had 'sold out' to other members of the EU as a bargaining ploy to gain other advantages was bound to gain currency in that environment. The levels of confusion over what action to take and what the future would hold also served to deepen local suspicions about what was happening. There were rumours that the government knew during the previous autumn that Foot and Mouth was in the country and that stockpiles of railway sleepers on which to burn the carcasses had been being built up over a period of months before the official outbreak. I personally heard accounts of infected carcasses being driven for hundreds of miles across the country supposedly to transport them to the nearest disposal site and of individuals being encouraged to keep quiet about their own suspicions. In other words there was a powerful atmosphere of mistrust that was readily exacerbated by the unfolding events. However, it also seemed to me that part of the problem was that the genuine commitment of farmers to their stock and the nature of the relationships between many owners and their animals could find no way of being articulated and acknowledged within the official processes.

On the one hand farming was being presented as a purely commercial activity within which animals were simply numbers on a piece of paper to be disposed of without any further consideration, or else there were a few errant farmers and other hangers-on who displayed an outdated and inappropriate sentimental attachment to animals that bore no relationship to the realities of the commercial world. Although I can see that there were individuals who fitted either one or other of those extremes I would argue that what I encountered as I spoke to farmers was a real concern for these other lives for which they carried a responsibility. Even though this would end in the death of these animals for food and in an essential commercial exchange there was still a level of relationship that could not simply be reduced to money or statistics. Our culture seems unable to recognize this level of human response, one that I believe fits the description of pre-autonomous. Part of it certainly derives from the time and effort that farmers 'invest' in the care of their livestock. This is neither simply a financial investment nor an emotional or sentimental one. It is more about 'being with' and sharing space and time. For some this is of no significance but for others it creates a relationship that it is very difficult to articulate let alone quantify. I still believe that some of the anti-government feeling that was expressed by the farming community resulted from this failure to acknowledge the pre-autonomous dimension of the events.

Another aspect that was regularly registered in both private and public discussions with farmers was a failure of government to realize that, for many, farming was not simply another source of employment, but a way of life or even a vocation. As a priest I could identify with these feelings. For those who were running family farms and faced the threat of having nothing to pass on to their children or that their children would not consider following into the family business, the events were a direct challenge to their sense of identity. Again, there was an 'investment' in farming that could not be reduced to finance and that would require a sacrifice of family identity that government appeared either unable or unwilling to acknowledge. I am not arguing that this should have been a decisive factor in the decisions taken, nor am I saying that there are not other industries that have had a similar influence upon people's lives, but what I do argue is that the failure to acknowledge this dimension of human subjectivity exacerbated the tensions between farmers and government. Simply to respond to these events at the level of autonomy, presenting the solutions as justified by a supposedly objective scientific approach, is to leave out reference to a whole layer of human response. This is a cultural problem though and cannot solely be laid at the door of any one administration. My own local attempts to allow and encourage farmers to articulate their feelings and frustrations would, I am sure, be labelled as purely 'pastoral' and therapeutic and thus of no further significance. The group that convened on a number of occasions to share the experiences were able to move on to discuss matters of politics and reorganization once the other level had been brought to the surface. The two levels are intimately connected and to deal with one at the expense of the other is to adhere to a reduced understanding of what it is to be a human being.

The impact of the mass cull of stock which took place during the first half of 2001 went well beyond the farmers themselves. I am not now thinking of the economic implications for the tourist industry, although I would want to acknowledge that this was a significant aspect of what happened and that a number of rural businesses were badly affected by the closure of areas of our most attractive countryside. I am thinking of the other inhabitants of some of our villages, those perhaps not quite so used to the darker side of rural life but accustomed to getting in their cars and commuting to work because of the accessibility of motorways and transport systems. While some parts of the countryside are still predominantly farming communities, others such as ours are a mixture and farming is simply one network amongst many. Children from the farms attend the local school and make friends with children from the new estate who may not have a rural background of any sort. One of the failures of imagination during our worst period was to realize that the farm on which stock were about to be slaughtered and burned was right next door to the new estate and just down the road from the local primary school. Those in charge of the cull and subsequent fires gave no warning to either of the other parties that this was about to happen. The men in white coats just appeared, the sounds of shots being fired and animals being killed rang out over the village and the school had to make a decision to close down because of the fears over the smoke coming out of the funeral fires. There was considerable distress amongst the younger families that this could suddenly happen without any warning and that parents were faced with explaining to their young children why the animals they had been taken to see the day before were now being shot. Once again I am not resorting to sentimentality here but I am arguing that part of what makes us human is the way in which we treat other life – that is why parents take their children to see the animals – so the actions of those days including the subsequent fires that burnt for about two weeks need to be questioned. Even if the cull was the appropriate response, the way in which it was handled in our locality left much to be desired. I will refer back to this episode later in the chapter.

The role of the experts within the process has already been mentioned, but also has a further dimension to it. One of the staggering accounts from the locality was that of the MAFF official who turned up at the end of the drive of one of our local residents under orders to come on site and cull some sheep. The information that he had received was correct in that there were indeed sheep belonging to that family, but incorrect in that he thought he was coming on to a farm. This particular property had ceased being a farm a generation earlier. The maps and the data on which the officials were operating had clearly not been updated despite frequent demands to farmers to provide information about all of their activities in order to access potential subsidies. A number of farmers were somewhat curious to know what had happened to all this information that they had been pressured to produce when it was obvious that the officials appeared to have no knowledge of it. This particular operative had been seconded from Walsall Town Centre because they were so short of staff, and had absolutely no experience of farming. He could not enter the property himself until a qualified vet arrived so he sat at the foot of this drive reading his paper and eating his sandwiches for about three days before a vet appeared. The family involved who had bred this small flock over a period of 25 years were faced with the agonizing decision of whether to fight the order to cull on the grounds that they were not contiguous with an outbreak – which they were not according to any sane assessment – or to allow the cull to happen before their ewes went into lamb on the basis that their appeal would be a waste of time anyway and they would go through the trauma of lambing simply to have the stock put down. They made the painful decision to allow the cull to happen, but without believing that the action was justified. There were similar stories of individuals attempting to fight the central directives and ultimately having to agree to meaningless compromises in order to keep the officials 'happy'.

In other words, the actual processes carried out once the decisions had been taken were often inept and inconsistent. Large amounts of money went into certain pockets, notably those who provided the slaughtermen and the subsequent clear-up operations while farmers were left contemplating whether or not they had a future in the industry. Vets from other countries who had no knowledge of the locality or its people were brought across to carry out these unenviable tasks because the departments had been cut back by successive administrations and did not have the staff to cope. Some staff were themselves under immense pressure and close to breaking point as our Chaplain to Agriculture and Rural Life testified at the time. The big problem here, in addition to lack of resources, was a failure and refusal to take seriously local knowledge. Once again this was presented as a conflict between the 'experts' who were carrying out their tasks in a rational, objective and scientific manner and the locals whose judgements were clouded by sentiment and local relationships. The idea that farmers themselves might know something about what they were dealing with never seemed to occur to some officials and was given no credence in government circles. This is not simply a debate between pre-autonomy and autonomy but about the existence of 'reason' – if that is what it is – at different levels in a culture and the ways in which 'experts' disenfranchise those with local knowledge. It is clear though that this failure was another contributory factor to the conspiracy theories that abounded amongst the farming population. Was this accidental incompetence or deliberate plan? It is perhaps impossible to resolve this question.

What I intend to do now is to draw upon some theoretical resources in order to show how the notion of autonomy can be both critiqued and then further developed. Given that the Foot and Mouth outbreak raised what are primarily environmental issues and questions of how the human is related to non-human nature it is this investigation into human subjectivity that is most relevant. However, this is a necessary extension of our concern to understand how it might be possible to move towards the open identity that I believe is the appropriate Christian response to globalization.

Deconstructing autonomy

I have already suggested that from within the four criteria for 'eating well' identified earlier it will be in the area of human subjectivity where we encounter the ideas required for this discussion. The concept of human autonomy is often cast as the villain of the piece by environmentalists when it comes to thinking about our relationships with non-human nature. The question arises as to whether this can be deconstructed or shown to contain other possibilities which could lead to drawing the boundaries between human and human and indeed human and non-human in a different way. I will argue that this is in fact the case and that it is in the debate about human identity that we discover the deepest challenges presented by environmental issues. In order to do this I will draw upon the work of three philosophers, Derrida, Levinas and Irigaray. Their work is of value, not because it presents us with understandings of human identity that are to be uncritically adopted, but because it serves to open up other possibilities for relatedness that give critical perspectives on the notion of autonomy.

I turn once again to the work of Derrida. I have argued elsewhere (Reader 2002, 88), that this is required if we are to establish a counter-point to Habermas's arguments in his treatment of the unconscious and also the affective and subjective dimensions of what it is to be a human being. Even though Habermas claims to have done justice to these within his theories of communicative reason, discourse ethics and deliberative democracy, his view of human subjectivity remains essentially rationalistic and cognitive. He appears to hold that individual persons, by reflecting more deeply and critically upon themselves, using the techniques of therapy or of self-awareness derived from the stages of human development, should be capable of countering the pathologies or distortions of human behaviour and communication. One can argue that this is too one-sided a view of human nature and denies the extent to which other areas of our subjective functioning remain either a mystery or, at least, resistant to articulation and manipulation. Derrida, on the other hand, is always more realistic at drawing out that which remains beyond articulation, be it through a Freudian concept of the unconscious or the unidentified factors behind human motivation. By doing this he identifies the possible limits of autonomy and provides a realistic counter-balance to Habermas's continuing optimism.

However, Derrida's critique goes much deeper than this by suggesting that there is a level of human functioning which is pre-autonomous and that what we call reason has actually been determined by such pre-autonomous encounters (Derrida 1999, 26). It is here that we find the most significant challenge to the boundaries of human identity as drawn by Habermas. In a major text which explores the nature of religion itself (Derrida and Vattimo 1998), Derrida attempts to show that there is the possibility of a deeper level of connection between reason and religion than either is prepared to acknowledge. Before there can be either reason or religion both will have had to respond to what Derrida terms the pre-autonomous encounter with the other. Only once this has occurred do what we call reason and religion begin to form, and then invariably now in apparent opposition to each other as this is what current culture demands. Thus both reason, operating for instance in the guise of science, and religion, as adherence to a tradition or institution, presuppose a trust or confidence in a particular way of working or seeing the world. They already rest upon an encounter with what might appear to be an ontological commitment before they can begin to function. So there has to be a trust in human reason, for instance, that cannot itself be justified according to reason, before one can pursue the scientific path. This is a form of faith in the way that things are, just as somebody displaying a religious commitment has a faith in the way that life is before they begin to develop that from within a tradition or community. There is a structure of human functioning, a pre-autonomous encounter with a way of looking at the world or maybe even with another person whom one implicitly trusts, that is common to both reason and religion. The latter may involve the singularity of a religious experience or encounter, but the former may equally rest upon the singularity of an encounter with a person or a moment of inspiration or 'revelation'. Only once these have occurred do the separate traditions we call reason and religion then come into play and take on a more structured form. Trust lies at the very heart of both encounters and in fact precedes what is normally presented as human autonomy – a deliberately and carefully chosen course of action or belief based on independent thought and reflection. Autonomous decision comes after the encounter with the other and, in fact, there can be no decision until after that encounter has taken place. This is the case for both reason and religion.

If such an explanation is to be accepted, then this does not deny that there is a genuine role for human reason as described by Habermas, as this would follow on from the pre-autonomous encounter, but it does point out that every approach

101

to questions of meaning has to begin somewhere. Even Habermas's concept of communicative reason can only function if one has already accepted his particular notion of truth, and this would have to be a matter of trust rather than of explicit reasoning. The same structure is at work in what we more readily identify as matters of faith. It is also to be found in the development of relationships between individual human beings. It may well be the very first moment of eye contact between two individuals that sets the tone for and determines the subsequent relationship. Without that point of contact there may be no further relationship. No conscious choices are being made at this point as the individuals may not even be aware that there is something happening, but without that dynamic of contact and response there can be no relationship. This part of the process is pre-verbal and pre-autonomous.

Once the initial point of contact has been made and a relationship develops through the channel of verbal communication, then one is in the realm of Habermas's communicative reason and the criteria for effective communication can come into action. However, this now acknowledges that there is a level of human functioning which cannot be fully captured by or encapsulated within language. It would also suggest that this dimension of human encounter, whether it is with another human being or with the other that is a singularity of experience, is beyond the conscious and deliberate control that we term autonomy.

How might this be of significance for our particular concerns? The first point is that it is an acknowledgment that although human beings may indeed exercise degrees of autonomy, we are not simply or exclusively autonomous in the sense of always exercising conscious control over choices and decisions. The pre-autonomous level is clearly of importance in the way that we understand how humans function both in relationships and in terms of adopting ideas and perspectives. We also operate at a level over which we have much less, if any, conscious control, and this may go some way to determining and shaping our subsequent actions. So the boundaries of human identity need to be drawn in such a way as to take this level of human functioning into account.

I would also want to suggest that if this pre-autonomous level of operation is of significance for our relationships with other humans, then it may also be of significance for our relationships with non-human nature. This may be more difficult to articulate simply because such points of encounter are not subsequently turned into direct communication through language, but it is perhaps one way of thinking about human responses to the external world as often expressed through the arts or music. Human beings are more sensitive to and influenced by their surroundings, the sights, sounds, smells and touch of other life, than we tend to acknowledge. However, this level of operation is more difficult to build into the worlds of either science or politics, which is where we are more likely to play out the practical implications of our relationships with non-human nature.

It is one thing to have the subjective experience of being 'at one with' the natural world, but it is entirely another to work out how, or even why, this could have any impact upon environmental legislation or even one's own personal attitudes towards certain issues. These are, after all, just 'feelings', and therefore not to be taken into account when hard choices and decisions have to be made. The boundary between objective and subjective, between the 'others' of reason and reason, held so sharply and firmly, automatically excludes the pre-autonomous level from our political processes. This is not to suggest however that all our problems would be solved if we were willing or able to acknowledge this pre-rational level of human functioning, for this could merely represent a regression to a more 'primitive' level of being. It does tell us though that a clearly-bounded concept of autonomy can and does need to be questioned and that it is possible to develop a more complex understanding of human identity.

Levinas

I turn now to a brief exploration of some ideas of Levinas. Although he died in 1996, it is only in the last few years that his work has begun to figure widely in either philosophy or theology. One suspects that 'his time has now come' – at least for a while – and that there will be increasing reference to his writings. It has been argued (Critchley and Bernasconi [ed.] 2002, 1), that his Jewish background and the fact that he lost significant numbers of his family during the Holocaust is a determining factor in his thinking. Certainly his emphasis upon ethics as first philosophy, and that being based upon the face-to-face encounter with the other person leading to an unconditional and non-reciprocal responsibility, stems from the failings in human relationships revealed by those devastating events. In many ways all of his philosophical writing is the outworking of these central ideas, but there is a clear process of development in his work.

His first major publication, *Totality and Infinity* (Levinas 1969) aroused both interest and criticism. It was Derrida, in a now famous essay (Derrida 1997), who suggested that Levinas fell into the trap of trying to articulate a pre-ontological experience – that of the face-to-face encounter with the other eliciting the response of care – in what was still ontological language. In his second major text *Otherwise Than Being* (Levinas 1981), Levinas appears to have accepted this criticism and now knowingly and explicitly attempts the impossible of saying what cannot be said, acknowledging that the language we use cannot escape certain ontological presuppositions. It is this later work that I will draw upon here. It is also worth noting that both Derrida and Levinas stand broadly within the phenomenological tradition, hence their shared interest in those experiences of the world mediated by our senses that are neglected by more cognitively-based philosophers such as Habermas. However, they are also aware of the limitations of phenomenology and, in particular, any attempts to argue directly from these sense experiences to philosophical conclusions. It is a point that needs to be carefully watched in the work both of Levinas and also of Irigaray, who shares this philosophical heritage.

Returning then to Levinas's reaction to the Holocaust, he expresses the concern that we can fail to acknowledge the humanity of the other person wherever that other is reduced to a faceless number or to a means to an end. His initial response to this, however, involved the familiar ideas of reviving reciprocity, symmetry, equality and recognition within human relationships. In other words, recognizing the other as the same as oneself, as another human being worthy of equal respect, was deemed to be sufficient to ground the moral response to inhumane activity. It was the inadequacy of this language to express the singularity of the encounter with the other to which Derrida drew attention in his critique of *Totality and Infinity*. Hence in his later work Levinas struggles constantly to abandon reciprocity and symmetry and to try to find ways of expressing and describing the infinite demands placed upon each of us by the other person. The language that he uses for this is often stark and apparently unreasonable, giving an extreme meaning to otherwise familiar terms such as hospitality, hostage, substitution and proximity. These are Levinas's attempts to push language beyond the boundary of comfortable and polite social discourse in order to say what cannot normally be said.

Before I offer brief examples of these I want to raise the question of whether these terms or ideas could be extended beyond human relationships into relationships with the non-human world. I am aware that Levinas himself did not suggest this and that only one other person, as far as I know (Llewelyn 1991), has expressed a similar suggestion. However, it seems to me a possible progression and worth considering. All I want to argue at this stage is that Levinas does provide another insight into the limitations of human autonomy and that therefore there are other possibilities for where we draw the boundaries of human identity.

The problem with the old familiar and relatively comfortable terminology of reciprocity, equality and recognition in human relationships is that, despite its support for notions of democracy and justice, it failed to prevent the atrocities of the Holocaust. This would be Levinas's challenge to the likes of Habermas and Rawls today. This language does not go far enough in portraying the absolute and unconditional nature of one's ethical responsibility for the other person. Hence we are in the realms of the tension between singularity or particularity and the universality of reason once again. The problem of the normal discourse of justice is that it turns the singularity of the direct encounter into abstractions and concepts thereby risking denying the humanity it claims to protect. There is of course a challenge the other way round, that of how to turn the singularities into structures of law, justice and ethical codes. I believe that the task is to try not to evade this tension but to allow space for the validity of both approaches.

Levinas's concerns lead him to suggest that there is a pre-original level of human functioning, similar to Derrida's idea of the pre-autonomous encounter with the other. So it is not that one consciously or deliberately chooses to take responsibility for another having first encountered the other person. The language of choice already comes too late upon the scene. One always already has that responsibility for the other person because one is passive with regard to the approach of the other. This may seem unreasonable, but that is the whole point of what Levinas is saying. According to the norms of justice and of civilized society one's responsibility for the other is entirely unreasonable:

> The unlimited responsibility in which I find myself comes from the hither side of my freedom, from a 'prior to every memory', an 'ulterior to every accomplishment', from the non-present par excellence, the non-original, the an-archical, prior to or beyond essence. (Levinas 1981, 10)

The basis for the encounter with the other is not some predetermined social structure but that of the most direct and unmediated experience. One is 'exposed' to the other, very much as the skin is exposed to what can wound it. One encounters the other not as an object disclosed by some theory but in a defenceless passivity where one cannot even protect oneself from the other person's presence or their infinite demands. Levinas talks about the exposure to the other as disinterestedness, proximity, an obsession by the neighbour despite one's own intentions (Levinas 1981, 55). So this is something beyond consciousness where one is already a substitution for the other and finds oneself a hostage for the other. His way of describing proximity is particularly powerful:

> Proximity is not a state, a repose, but a restlessness, null site, outside of the place of rest. It overwhelms the calm of the non-ubiquity of a being which becomes a rest in a site. No site then is ever sufficiently a proximity, like an embrace. Never close enough, proximity does not congeal into a structure, save when represented in the demand for justice as reversible, and reverts into a simple relation. (Levinas 1981, 82)

Proximity precedes subjectivity, not the other way around. So one does not become aware of oneself and then subsequently discover oneself in 'proximity' with another. The proximity is rather a condition for becoming aware of oneself at all. One can see from this what Levinas is trying to get at, but can also recognize the difficulties of trying to express this in language which presupposes the very structure of relationships he is trying to bring into question. Levinas's own way of expressing this tension – as we have already seen – is to talk about both the Saying and the Said (Levinas 1981, 43). The Saying is the performative act, the direct and unmediated encounter which can only happen because the relationship of proximity or responsibility already exists prior to any conscious decision or choice. The Said is the inevitable articulation of this encounter which, although essential, can only fail to do justice to the reality of the Saying simply because the language we use tends

105

to reduce the other to the same and thus to objectify the other. It is impossible to avoid the reduction of the Saying to the Said, but the task must always be to bring to the surface the residue of the Saying that rests within the Said in order to prevent it compromising the spirit of responsibility within relationship to which Levinas is trying to point.

The theological overtones of Levinas's ideas are surely clear enough. The primacy of the face-to-face encounter as the basis for any ethics has its attractions for a Christian approach, although it may lead to an extreme interpretation which leaves little room for a collective or institutionalized response. The same may be said of the language he uses to describe the pre-autonomous encounter. Words such as hostage, proximity and welcome, in the way that he employs them, appear destined to make a point and then to leave one searching for more structured means of relating to others. Nevertheless, the tension between the Saying and the Said that dominates his later work is undoubtedly an important one for the world of faith and deepens the concern to look beyond the familiar concept of autonomy in order to identify other ways of understanding human subjectivity. If the power of articulation is indeed so limited, then how can relationships be represented in the public domain?

As I have already suggested, there must be questions about what Levinas is trying to say. Is he proposing what is really an impossible ideal of relationship, a depth of responsibility that will be so overwhelming and demanding that anyone is likely to shy away from any level of care or commitment to another person? Does he fail to take full account of the role of human agency and decision by placing so much emphasis upon a pre-originary or pre-conscious level? If all response is simply pre-autonomous in this way what scope is there for human growth and development, or those further levels of self-awareness and enlightenment which may be valid goals for human identity and relationship? However, despite these significant doubts, I repeat my argument that Levinas's ideas, alongside those of Derrida, do provide a critical counter-point to the notion that humans are simply and exclusively autonomous. It may still be worth pondering, at some future point, the extent to which the notions of proximity, hostage, substitution and hospitality might be extended to human relationships with the natural world and thus further help to question the boundaries that we tend to draw between the two. Have we yet acknowledged the depth to which we are always already in relationship with non-human nature, even if we subsequently reduce this to a means-ends relationship? If not the end of a different account of these relationships it is at least perhaps another beginning.

Irigaray
As we move on to consider the work of Luce Irigarary it becomes clear that she takes even further the questioning of familiar boundaries begun by Derrida and Levinas. Although she is explicitly critical of both of them (Irigaray 2000a, 35) as not being

able to acknowledge the centrality of sexual difference, there is no doubt that she is still building upon their ideas. Recognized essentially as a leading contribution to feminist philosophy, Irigaray's work is now being translated into English and thus more readily available. Irigaray continues to develop her own thinking although there is clear continuity between her earlier and later work. The objective in this section is simply to draw attention to those parts of her writings that deepen the reflection upon notions of autonomy and to draw out her radical suggestions for an understanding of human identity.

That there could be such a thing as sexual difference rests at the heart of her recent work (Irigaray 1996, 47). I deliberately phrase it that way because Irigarary does not say that it is possible to identify sexual difference from within current beliefs and practices, but instead tries to show that this is exactly not what is ever explicitly acknowledged but may remain as an open possibility. In this sense she is close to Derrida's use of deconstruction, analysing what does exist in order to draw out the other hidden or suppressed possibilities. However, unlike Derrida, she refrains from articulating what that other possibility would be. Rather, in the manner of Levinas, she takes existing language to its extreme and beyond in order to display both its limits and its 'other' possibilities.

She argues that Western philosophy constantly reduces the other to the same – even Levinas is accused of making this mistake – by refusing to recognize that, in the difference between male and female genders, we should be talking about Two not One. Even though we do not yet have the language to express this adequately, Irigaray insists that the differences between male and female are such that we are talking here about a new ontology. To this point ontology deals with the One and the Many, thus reducing all being to the same, but what it cannot do is to acknowledge that there is the One and the Other, thus the Two – male and female. What would be there as the Other (the second or female if one is male) is constantly drawn back into the masculine dominated terminology. Hence this is more than just saying, in the manner of Derrida and Levinas, that what is required is respect for difference and otherness, because even this is to reduce the Other to the same or to the One. The Other is so other as to demand a language and an ontology that has yet to be developed. Instead of a singularity of one Irigarary is pointing to a singularity of two. As I said, she is stretching language beyond its breaking point because in this lies the only hope of change and the possibility of re-drawing the boundaries of human identity.

These differences are themselves visible in the different ways that men and women use language. Women privilege intersubjectivity; the relationship with the other gender; ways of being two; the physical and natural environment and the present and future tenses. Men, on the other hand, privilege the subject-object relation; the production of pieces of work rather than respect for the world as it is;

the use of instruments; the relationship between the one and the many; the representation of the universe as made up of abstractions and the past tense (Irigaray 2000b, 15). One major explanation for this is that women create in themselves, within their own bodies, whereas men can only create externally. Belonging to the two different genders then is seen to be determinative of language, conceptual thought and even political structures. Irigaray is clear that both families and civil society need to be re-ordered in order to take account of the possibilities of sexual difference.

All of this has implications both for the familiar concept of autonomy and for human relationships with the natural world. Within the masculine mode autonomy is associated with control by means of domesticating, taming and conquering. This control is extended beyond relationships with women to control over the natural world as object to be shaped and manipulated. What is called for is a new autonomy, one that renounces the aggression and violence towards the other, and instead allows the other to exist as different rather than trying to reduce her to the same. Similarly, in relationships with the natural world, nature must be allowed to be as it is, rather than being reduced to objects that are merely of instrumental value. It would seem then that Irigarary is very close to the romantic version of postmodernity that simply accepts the cultural dichotomy between reason and the 'others' of reason, with what is female and also of the natural world identified with the 'others' of reason. However, this would be to attribute to her an essentialism which is, in fact, one of the targets of her critique. She portrays women and nature in this way not in order to argue that this is their essential nature but to show that these portrayals are the inevitable consequence of the failure to think sexual difference.

In a major commentary upon Irigaray's later work, Penelope Deutscher draws out this radical dimension of her thought (Deutscher 2002, 107). Irigaray does not intend to reify sexual difference in traditional terms, thus leaving women identified with the emotional, the natural, the bodily and therefore the irrational – all the 'others' of reason. To see women as other is not to see them as 'not-men', just lacking the masculine qualities (Irigaray 2000b, 15). However, she does not propose an alternative essence of woman because it has been made impossible for women and men to have separate subjectivities. It is this impossibility which suggests that there could be an alternative configuration of male and female subjectivities so, as Deutscher says, Irigaray presents us with a set of open brackets or just a question mark. When she refers to the feminine she is not talking about even a buried or repressed truth, nor is she giving content to a new utopian possibility of femininity. We do not know what sexual difference is, we only know that it might exist by the signs that it does not. This means that everything Irigaray writes, whether about women or about relationships with the natural world, although they may sound as if they are offering a positive content, are not in fact intended to do that at all. Yet this is the best that can be done in the circumstances, reminding us of the tension between the Saying and the Said in Levinas's work.

On the matter of boundaries, Irigaray is eager to warn against the dangers of appropriating the other, of subsuming difference within the same. Women themselves fall into this trap in their relationships with lovers and children because they have not yet learnt or developed other ways of relating. One needs to remember that who the other person is for me is not who they are for themselves. To assume otherwise is to consume the other person and to reduce them to the same. So what is required is an ethics of non-appropriation. However, as Deutscher points out, this seems like an impossibility if there is to be real relationship (Deutscher 2002, 80). Perhaps Irigarary's position demands too clear a definition of boundaries and ignores the inevitable crossing and blurring that is essential in real relationship. At this point it is possible that Irigaray tries to be too prescriptive in her writing, trying to determine what sexual difference would look like in practice. Perhaps this reflects the impossibility of trying to express what is simply an impossibility, and the constant temptation to feed positive content into such a discussion.

In this most difficult of tasks we encounter one of the other locations where I have suggested that reason and the 'others' of reason may encounter one another, the realm of the messianic. Sexual difference as it functions in Irigaray's work appears to be a messianic concept. We do not yet know what it is, but we can believe it is still to come. Even if it did arrive we might not be able to recognize it. If we felt that we had recognized it we would most likely be mistaken in any case. Yet the idea is required in order to keep us moving from where we are now towards other possibilities. So the messianic is not to be confused nor identified with any specific messianism; it remains a matter of anticipation, of empty brackets or a question mark. The actual nature of this identity and the re-drawing of the boundaries within relationships must remain an open possibility.

It is here I think that Irigaray takes the argument beyond the point reached by Derrida and Levinas. Their particular contribution has been to open up the concept of autonomy by drawing out a pre-autonomous or pre-rational level of human operation. With Irigaray we are pointed towards an impossibility which lies beyond autonomy, or perhaps towards new forms of autonomy. To the extent to which philosophers such as Habermas hold a concept of autonomy which is derived from a masculine approach, thus focusing on the control of the 'others' of reason in order to counter possible pathologies and to allow reason to operate unhindered, they remain bound within the Enlightenment paradigm. Without something like the messianic concept of sexual difference they are not going to be able to move beyond or to critique the restricting concept of autonomy.

It is not perhaps so easy to translate Irigaray's ideas into the theological domain but there are some points of connection. The continuing attempts to redefine relationships between men and women are a difficult but essential area for Christian debate, although Irigaray's suggestions may be on the radical end of the spectrum. However, the question of how to establish a proper respect between women and men can readily be extended to human relationships with the non-human order. The messianic dimension of her thought is of considerable significance and I will return to this in the conclusion. The question of the possibility of an ethics of non-appropriation is an important one, although again, as with elements in Levinas's thought it may appear to be a little too extreme when it comes to the practice of relationships rather than the ideal.

However, I believe that our encounter with the work of these three writers shows us the value of deconstructing autonomy in order to assist in the process of drawing the boundaries between human and non-human in a different way, but would also want to claim that what is required now is a reconstruction that opens up new possibilities for identity and relationship. Derrida, Levinas and Irigaray offer different but effective counter-points and correctives to Habermas's reconstruction of reason, not giving us cause to abandon his project, but ways to extend it into other areas.

Conclusions

I have been arguing that a major contribution that these philosophers can offer as we struggle with some of the practical involvements of a broadly environmental nature is a reconfiguration of the concept of human autonomy. However, such a reconfiguration requires not an outright rejection of this concept but rather an extension of it to include consideration both of the pre-autonomous levels identified by Derrida and Levinas and of the possible new autonomies yet to be developed as suggested by Irigaray. In order to illustrate that something like Habermas's concept of communicative reason is still required and also to move the discussion towards a programme of further research I want to refer back to our practical example.

I have already suggested how singularities, direct personal experiences of other possibilities for relating and the drawing of boundaries, might influence structured behaviour and institutional responses, and I believe that this example will reinforce the importance of this. This incident took place during the outbreak of Foot and Mouth Disease. As already mentioned there is no doubt that the sounds of animals being shot coupled with the sights and smells of burning carcasses had a deep effect not only upon the farming community but also upon other local residents. One such site for slaughter was right next door to the new housing estate on which live a number of young families (i.e. with children under nine years old). On one of the mornings when I was doing my regular visit to the Mothers and Toddlers group in the village, surrounded by an apparently idyllic 'pastoral' scene of mothers and offspring playing and chatting happily, it came to me that just a few yards down the road we (i.e. humans) were in the process of slaughtering other mothers and their offspring (these were sheep during the lambing season).

It is impossible to describe the full impact of this, but there was a moment when I felt I would have to leave the room because the pain and knowledge of this was unbearable. It would be easy from the outside to describe this as pure sentimentality. I can only say that this experience was not of that order. For a few moments the normal boundaries between human and non-human were breached and it appeared to me that the differences we create in our minds between 'different' beings are arbitrary to the point of meaninglessness. To say that these are merely animals and that it does not matter what we do to them was a violation of life of all kinds. I was not 'at one with' the natural world, but I caught a glimpse of a different location for the human within it.

As I have said, this was a personal experience, a singularity, and there is no doubt that others have similar experiences which trigger feelings about the possibility of another relationship with the 'natural world'. This was perhaps of the order of the pre-autonomous encounters identified by Derrida and Levinas. The question is that of what differences these may make to what we do in practice. I would argue that until or unless they can be translated into a structural or institutional change they remain of limited significance. How might an incident such as the one described, for instance, have an impact upon political legislation? I contacted both Downing Street directly and MAFF as it then was, with my pastoral concerns for the 'feelings' of farmers involved which were never taken into account in the action that was sanctioned, and simply received the stock press release about the need for a restructuring of agriculture in this country and in Europe. But then this is the whole problem: the deep emotions aroused by these events had no way of being fed into the public debate or political processes because such 'feelings' are seen as the 'other' of reason and can find no acknowledgement in the decision making. However, the reality is that such 'feelings' do affect our decisions whether we acknowledge it or not, but that we try to pretend otherwise through rationalization or by objectifying what is happening.

In Levinasian terms, how can the Saying – the direct personal experience – affect the Said – the public articulation of events ? How can the inevitably inaccurate articulations or singularities be introduced into the level of public discourse in ways that might change how we respond and react? Yet unless there is also a type of communicative reason, a shared understanding of how language functions that establishes criteria for effective communication, how can this affective level of human functioning be acknowledged within the process of decision making? The pre-autonomous needs to be acknowledged within the apparently autonomous in order for this to happen and so the boundaries of what constitute human identity need to be re-drawn.

111

Yet if we are to take seriously Irigaray's suggestion that what is now required is a new form of autonomy, there must be the possibility of moving beyond existing notions of this concept while acknowledging both the pre-autonomous and the autonomous dimensions of human subjectivity. The challenge, as Irigaray sometimes, but not always points out, is of how to begin to articulate what this means without falling into the trap of circumscribing this by the use of current language and concepts. It is when Irigaray herself starts to articulate what either sexual difference or the new autonomy might look like that she transgresses her own self-imposed limits and strays into the realm of the messianic. In other words, whatever this new autonomy or post-autonomy might be, as soon as one begins to flesh it out with specific content, it fails to do justice to the messianic vision that it claims to espouse. How might it be possible to keep the content of this new identity open enough to prevent falling into this trap and yet specific enough to provide a horizon against which to evaluate current action? We have already seen that the question of identity formation has been highlighted by writers such as Castells (Castells 1997) drawing out the impact of the forces of globalization upon individuals from within the field of sociology. Where one draws the boundaries between human and non-human and indeed how one establishes the contours of one's individual identity are both fluid and negotiable processes. The problems appear to arise as and when particular people or groups attempt to respond to the forces of rapid change by retreating behind a determinate or fixed identity. This reaction is understandable but can lead, in its most extreme form, to a fundamentalist response to all change. This can happen within religious traditions such as Christianity but can also appear in the guise of a retreat to a pre-autonomous level of operation that is to be found within some environmental movements. The question then is that of how to encourage and foster the construction of a more open identity, one that does not seek to predetermine the direction in which humanity is going while yet not being so indeterminate as to accept any change irrespective of its consequences. It is here that some insights from the Christian tradition have something to offer.

First there is the idea that by following in the way of Christ one enters a new creation, a transformation of existing circumstances that can only dimly be glimpsed in the here and now. There is the (messianic) promise of a new world, a new order, one that is never wholly to be identified with a current situation. Although this may sound so indeterminate as to be of no practical use, it is clear that certain conditions must be met if this is to come about. Notions of justice, of care for the whole of the created order, of respect between different beings and different orders of being, all of these based upon the assumption that the creator's vision is one of a love that reunites and restores the whole of creation are fundamental to this promise. We may never fully know what this will mean in practice, but we can discern when certain developments are in conflict with this overall vision.

Second is the understanding that humans construct their identities from components that are contingent and temporary but that they have an innate tendency to portray these components as necessary and permanent. 'Who I am' can be clearly established according to recognizable criteria within any particular culture. Within the current culture largely determined by Western global capitalism, 'I' am identified by access to wealth, status, possessions and celebrity. 'I' am certainly defined by the work that I do, by my key personal relationships and by the freedoms that I claim to possess in directing and shaping my own life. There are additional components related to context and family, e.g. being a patron of the arts; supporting a particular football club; gaining qualifications or taking three holidays abroad each year, but all of these are seen as part of one's identity. Even those who resist such forces and try to establish alternative identities are still operating in the same manner. Part of what it seems to mean to be a human being is that one creates a sense of oneself as a distinct individual by combining components that one then portrays as being an essential part of oneself.

The Christian tradition surely offers each of us the promise of a new identity and a new way of being, neither of them constructed from these fleeting and ultimately untrustworthy components. It requires a letting go of all of these strands that we imagine combine to construct an identifiable person, a loss of self without which it is not possible to find that new world which has been promised to us. This is an open identity, one not formed nor predetermined by external factors, but which draws us onwards to that restoration of relationships that is the Kingdom of God. Our supposed 'possession' of ourselves, whether pre-autonomous or autonomous is a barrier to this development. Other traditions might express this by saying that the self is an illusion, but I prefer to think of the self as contingent and fleeting, estranged from the true self that we might become. It is in the light of these insights that we judge our current practice and beliefs.

So the future remains open and the vision of a post-autonomy is one way in which we can hold onto this messianic promise of a world yet to be revealed. As John D. Caputo says, drawing on St Augustine, we are creatures who remain a question to ourselves (Caputo 2001, 27). Linking the communicative reason of Habermas to the other levels of human subjectivity identified by Derrida, Levinas and Irigaray may help theology to recover the vision that it requires in order to argue for the messianic dimension of human relatedness to the non-human.

7

On the art of 'eating well'

The question of housing

To return to the beginning: if a young couple were to arrive on my doorstep today in need of housing what would I do, or what would I do differently from in 1987? I would know this time that I should refer them to the lettings officer of the local Housing Association who would be able to advise them how they might score under the current allocations system and how long they might have to wait to find suitable accommodation. I would be able to sympathize with the general plight of young couples being unable to live in their original communities but also be aware of a number of families who had successfully relocated into the local towns and made reasonable lives for themselves there. However, I would also know that this has a knock-on effect for the rural areas where the young families that do arrive have access to greater financial resources and exercise choices that might put facilities such as the school under threat. The sense of local identity and of loyalty that might have gone with that has been eroded to be replaced by a harder-edged consumerist approach to anything that the immediate locality has to offer. So there would be a sense of loss for things as they might have been running alongside a sense of the new opportunities that had been created by an influx of newcomers. But communities have always changed over time and this is simply the latest stage of the evolution. Within that the church has to work out where it stands and what role it has to play.

What about the more general issue of my involvement in the housing world as it is now? Given that this is one of the blurred encounters that dominates my current work have I now found a means of justifying this engagement? Certainly I would argue that housing continues to be a determining factor in the make up of our communities and both the problems and the possibilities in many people's lives. If anything I would argue that the need for church involvement now is even greater that it was in 1987. For instance, a government directive on recent planning guidance for this area of the West Midlands has determined that there is to be no more large scale housing development outside the arc of the Birmingham area.

Reasons given for this are the increased pressure on the transport infrastructure created by extra commuters and thus a need to prevent people moving further out into areas such as ours and overloading the motorway system. The drive to utilize brown field sites closer to the conurbation is all part of this proposal. Although this sounds a worthy and legitimate plan I understand from one local district councillor that they have had to withdraw 150 units of social housing from the local plan as a result and that to meet the current waiting list every proposed development in the district for the next ten years would have to be 100% social housing. The effect then is to put huge increased pressure on available development land, to make it even more difficult for Housing Associations to find any building land at all and to potentially deny smaller communities the opportunity of an influx of new people. Such a policy needs to be challenged at the highest level and its implications properly thought through.

If one adds to the national picture these particular local circumstances it becomes even more disturbing. There is a massive pressure on the South East and London for new housing. The projected growth in the number of households nationally between 1991 and 2016 is 4.4 million. Of these 3.5 million will be for single person households. This is the result of changing social and relationship patterns, notably women being prepared to live alone and preferring to do so and the increase in life expectancy. The current position in the South East is that even people who are earning reasonable professional salaries can no longer afford to enter the housing ownership market. In April 2004 the government put in place a 'key worker' scheme for professionals such as teachers and nurses to assist them to find accommodation in this part of the country. It is a real problem when such key workers cannot afford to live in an area as schools and hospitals will find it even harder to recruit staff. What we are seeing then is that the requirement for affordable housing will increase substantially over the coming years and that the potential role of Housing Associations will grow accordingly.

If one places this alongside the pressures that exist upon those who have been fortunate enough to enter the house-owning market, the need for both partners to work with the impact that has upon family and community life and work-life balance issues, then it is surely clear that the state of the housing market in this country is a major determinant of much of our social life. As we have seen locally through our experience with the Children's Festival and Toddlers group and the playgroup and school, who comes to live in the locality and what part, if any, they play in local activity and on what terms, is heavily influenced by what houses are built and at what price they are sold. All of this in itself would be quite enough to justify church involvement with housing issues, however there is now yet another strand to this argument.

The National Housing Federation – the umbrella body for Housing Associations – has recently launched a new initiative called InBusiness for Neighbourhoods. The document I referred to in the opening chapter is part of this initiative. The general argument about the increased pressure for affordable housing is very much as above, but combined with the need for Housing Associations to change their image and profile within national politics. Rather than being seen as a safety net for those who cannot buy their own properties, with all the stigma attached to that, the objective is to turn Housing Associations into springboards for creating sustainable neighbourhoods by encouraging them to get involved in a wider range of local activities. This is placed in the wider context of social and economic change in this country and their impact upon housing tenure. Interestingly it is now relationship insecurity that has replaced job insecurity as the major factor in the requirement for more affordable housing. Both of course are significant, with the influences of globalization running alongside those of changes in relationship patterns. The continuing decline of manufacturing industry and the leakage of jobs in the financial services sector to other countries leaves us as a nation where retail and distribution and public administration are the only growth sectors. As one commentator put it, we are becoming a nation of civil servants and bartenders (Scase 2004). China and India are experiencing rapid rates of economic growth and are now the major recipients of inward investment, whereas the European Union's share of world trade is stagnating or even declining. In other words we now face important questions about how we are going to generate income in the years ahead and therefore how we are going to pay for the growing demands on public services that currently form a vital topic for the political agenda. The view of some at least is that this is going to force the focus of social activity back down to neighbourhood level, and that levels of satisfaction are going to be based on the more familiar areas of friendship and community life. If this is true, so the argument goes, the Housing Associations are well-placed to play a key role in neighbourhood renewal and the encouragement of local social enterprise and civic leadership.

As I listened to this being proposed at a Housing Association gathering where the keynote speaker was Dr Richard Scase, one of the co-authors of the document on neighbourhood futures and of the National Housing Federation's strategy for the coming years, I wondered what part, if any, local churches might play in this developing scenario.

After all, if these projections are somewhere near the mark then they will have as much impact upon the local church as upon anybody else. This will be the environment in which we will be operating, but who is gathering this information on behalf of the churches let alone working out what its implications might be? The churches are still about the only institution left who maintain a presence in most local communities. Clergy still live in the locality whereas most other 'professionals' go back home at night and weekends. If Housing Associations have a crucial role to play in these developments then surely local churches also have an equally important task in 'creating sustainable neighbourhoods'? Is there not scope here for partnerships between Housing Associations and churches where and when they are major players in a local area? Can local churches become organized enough to get involved in this way? All of this suggests that the question of 'eating well', of crossing the boundary into welfare provision of various sorts while retaining a sense of identity and vision is going to become deeply significant over the next few years.

How then might we use the criteria suggested earlier to evaluate such potential involvement? Reminding ourselves that the locations for encounter are a common interest in the tension between the universal and the particular; the dimension of the messianic as a general structure of human life; a focus upon human subjectivity and particularly the drive for an open identity and finally an awareness of the degrees of uncertainty and indeterminacy that are part of both political and individual life, how might we use these to judge whether or not such an engagement between the church and housing world might be appropriate?

I believe that it should be clear by now that the tension between the universal and the particular cuts through the heart of contemporary concerns. The pressures of globalization within localities and individual lives are evident with the growing realization that different values or principles are in operation simultaneously. People claim that they want the advantages of local community, of local schools and facilities but will prefer to walk away from them and buy into better facilities elsewhere because they are afraid of losing out or falling behind in the competitive environment of the world of work. It is the universal of the global economy and its rules of operation creating pressure on individuals to establish their own successful lives without having reference to the older institutions that provided security and guidance that forms this structure for family and community life. However, a recognizable reaction against this 'invasion' by alien values into families and personal identity issues is to search for the 'enclaves of interim intimacy' which provide an illusion of the old-fashioned community where everybody knew everybody else and provided practical and emotional support in times of need. Churches readily become part of this counter-reaction against globalization and fall into this 'nostalgia trap', only to get a nasty shock when people choose to walk away from their latest projects because they get better value for money elsewhere. So what are we to do?

Given that we cannot but get involved, and inevitably become drawn into the creation of enclaves of interim intimacy we need to keep our heads above the water by retaining the messianic dimension of our activities and beliefs. Local projects are not an end in themselves, they are – or could be – a means of pointing us towards another goal, that which lies hidden beneath the details of individual relationships and points of tension within them, the personal development of the people who become engaged and the questions which they just might have to face as a result of this engagement. This represents the essential instability or chaos that is inescapably part of any human activity, the encounter with the other that Derrida helpfully portrays as deconstruction. Groups and communities that allow themselves to become enclosed and self-serving need to be challenged by such encounters, however they might occur, and I see a central part of the role of the church to provide locations for such encounters – hence the Children's Festival and the early stages of the Toddlers group. We have also seen the same principle at work in the discourses of human rights when they are at their most effective. However, all such projects rapidly form their own establishment, which in turn, need challenging and changing. Deconstruction then is a constant task and obligation and requires the introduction of new or destabilizing elements into any project.

Here then we can also see the importance of the other two criteria. If local churches were to become involved with Housing Associations in the task of creating sustainable neighbourhoods, they would need to retain their critical edge and not simply buy into what could be merely a dose of public rhetoric designed to serve other purposes. The understanding that what is always at stake in such projects is the self-questioning and potential development of the individuals concerned must be kept at the heart of the church's vision of what might be achieved. There is a real danger of neighbourhoods closing in upon themselves as a reaction to globalization and forming on the basis of some common interest or characteristic that then becomes the basis for an exclusivity. That may not be the intention, but it is always a risk and needs to be kept in the forefront of our minds. The test is how we respond to the other who does not fit our self-defined identity. Groups that become too comfortable are not going to cope well with such a challenge. Both the messianic concept of what it might mean to be human, as suggested in the previous chapter, and an awareness and openness to the indeterminacy and uncertainty of life are essential components of a Christian involvement in such social engagements. We may still get 'eaten' or appropriated because that is simply the cost of engagement, but at least we might be 'eaten well'.

On constructing an open identity

As I concluded at the close of the previous chapter it is inevitably speculative and dangerous to try to say too much about this subject even though it lies at the heart of what needs to be said. Whether one thinks about this in terms of Levinas's tension between the Saying and Said or in more traditional mystical language from the tradition of Christian spirituality, it is the territory towards which we should be constantly moving but which can only ever be a horizon for all our practical engagements. I want to return briefly though, to what we have learnt from our current local involvements about the human capacity to construct our identities from the components which our culture place before us, and to extend this into consideration of our necessary responses to others.

It is not that we can avoid creating a sense of ourselves or a personal identity or simply deny that this is a natural human task. From the earliest days we gain the impression that we are individual beings from the ways in which others treat and respond to us. One is given a name, a notion of belonging to a family or some particular social grouping and then proceeds to develop other aspects of one's identity building upon this foundation. It is on the basis of this sense of ourselves that we relate to others and receive back from them either confirmation or challenges to that identity. There are significant debates about the influences that gender might have upon how male and female form themselves differently, hence Irigaray's work upon the messianic concept of sexual difference. If she is correct about this then perhaps it is also possible that there could yet be an equivalent in terms of human relationships with the non-human world, a 'natural difference' that has yet to emerge but which remains as a horizon. However, we tend to approach our identity as if it were a given and work on the assumption that without it we could not get on in the world or form relationships with others.

There are interesting limit cases of this which might suggest that this concept of personal identity is more fragile and tenuous than we prefer to imagine. Those who work with people with dementia quickly realize that such individuals no longer hold that sense of themselves as personal memory recedes. They rely upon others to carry their stories and personal histories for them and require continuity and consistency of contact over time to have any structure of security. It is perhaps like a 'second childhood' in that individuals require somebody else to reflect back to them who they are or have been, but of course there is no process of development to follow and no opportunity to create a separate sense of self otherwise known as adulthood. This raises the question of whether such people are the ones who are closer to the ideal of an open identity, or whether one needs some base-line of self even in order to let go of that self.

Perhaps the most significant question is that of whether or not we make our judgements about ourselves and about others on the basis of these constructed characteristics. Is this really 'who I am', and are these personal characteristics what will define me in my relationships with others, including presumably for Christians, my relationship with God? Much of the evidence from our local projects would suggest that this is the way we think and operate. Whether one is part of a farming family which has lived and worked in an area for a long period, or a newcomer attempting to establish oneself with one's peer group by buying the right sort of house and driving the right sort of car and sending one's child to the right school, or whether one builds one's identity by belonging to the local football or cricket club, it is all very much the same process at work. Churches operate according to the same rules. Invariably we draw people in by giving them a sense of belonging or else by convincing them that this would be a good characteristic to add to their identity portfolio in some way. It would not be a good 'selling point' to present ourselves as the community which denies that there is any justifiable sense of community or identity. Yet perhaps this is the insight that lies at the heart of a Christian identity – self-emptying, self-giving or kenosis.

If it is true that God's love is indiscriminate and unconditional then that must mean it is available to each of us irrespective of those characteristics which create our sense of ourselves. It must also mean that we should offer to others as much of that love as we can muster irrespective of their characteristics: it does not matter who or what they or we think they are or what they have done, we are all God's creatures and worthy of love on that basis alone! This is too radical of course for normal human life since it means there are no boundaries, no means by which we can discriminate between our 'friends' and our 'enemies'. This is Derrida's unconditional hospitality and so far from everyday practice as to be another messianic horizon. It means that we are bound to welcome the other without knowing or caring who and what they are and thus risking the lives of our own group or loved ones.

> It is necessary to welcome the other in his alterity, without waiting, and thus not to pause to recognize his real predicates. It is thus necessary, beyond all perception, to receive the other while running the risk, a risk that it always troubling, strangely troubling, like the stranger, of a hospitality offered to the guest as ghost, or Geist or Gast. There would be no hospitality without the chance of spectrality. But spectrality is not nothing, it exceeds, and thus deconstructs, all ontological oppositions, being and nothingness, life and death – and it also gives… God without being, God uncontaminated by being – is this not the most rigorous definition of the Face of the Wholly Other? (Derrida 1997, 111–12)

This takes us well beyond the immediate and practical engagements which have been the main focus of this book and apparently a world away from Housing Associations and toddlers groups! Yet such ideas and insights do have to form the backdrop of our involvements if they are to avoid being appropriated by other agendas. If we are to realize the limitation of identifying ourselves and others according to the characteristics by which we construct a sense of ourselves then surely something similar might or must be at work in our relationship with and understanding of God. This is not to say that we will not paint into that open space some ideas, images or symbols which hopefully help us to relate, but that we must never forget that they are not the reality which we seek to penetrate. These are only proximate and contingent representations of that which cannot be represented. Similarly with our identity components and structures, they are not 'who we are' and should not be the ultimate base on which we relate to others or they to us. An open identity then is essential to the life of faith.

I want to mention another set of questions at this point. Not much work seems to have been done on the conditions which make it more likely or possible that individuals will develop a more open identity, and that I find surprising since it would offer a base line for Christian practical activity. What are the blocks and 'unblocks' towards the development of such an identity or what one might term a reflexive spirituality? Here are some suggestions.

First a safe space often presupposing a relationship of trust with a significant other person, perhaps building upon that pre-autonomous encounter with the other as referred to by Derrida and Levinas. I think we continue to underestimate the contribution of just being there alongside over a period of time and building up relationships that has been at the heart of parish life and is now being undermined by a series of internal and external forces. This is where interim intimacy is not enough and more consistent contact is what is required. How and where will this happen in a society that is so mobile and transitory? As people establish fleeting relationships using IT and the rapidly shifting world of work what are the implications for personal and spiritual growth? I think this is an unanswered question.

Second there needs to be an awareness of waiting for the other or the gift, the Messiah in Derrida's terms. If everything appears to be satisfactory as it is, or if one believes that one has 'made it', whatever that means, then there will be less openness to other possibilities and a decreased willingness to face up to destabilizing questions. There is something here about rich men going through eyes of needles I think. Apparent wealth or affluence is surely a potential barrier to further growth.

Third is the requirement for a discourse or sub-language in which to express those feelings or insights which form the singularities that often are the spur to growth. Again I think this is a real problem for a culture that has lost its religious discourse or traditions of spirituality and where people have to search for strands of language which perhaps do not cohere because of this lack of structure. Hence the telling of the stories of the tradition has a function in providing access to those potential resources.

Then finally there is something about knowing the right moment – the *kairos* – the point where something significant might change and somebody is ready to hear and respond. But then, the moment can so easily be lost and things go on as before.

If these are some of the 'unblocks' then one can see equally where the blocks will arise. Many of them are to do with the identity issues that we have examined in this book. It is when we think that we know who we are that we are least open to change and growth and much of our culture would try to persuade us that we do know just that because we have safely constructed our sense of self through commercial exchange and consuming both products and others in relationship. We need to learn to trust each other enough to move beyond this and once again admit that we do not know, but that we are called to remain a question to ourselves.

Postscript:
On a Christian encounter
with governance

I t is always very tempting to close a text simply by offering a section that is more obviously 'theological'. It feels neat and may stand a chance of pacifying those readers who might question whether or not there is enough explicit Christian content overall. Surely this is where one ought to end up in any case, by rounding off the argument or making the final point from within the tradition rather than from within another experience or discipline? However, this is a text about blurred boundaries where nothing is guaranteed to be where one might expect it and also where it is going to be difficult to bring the discussions to a neat conclusion in any case. So I have resisted the temptation to resort to what I call a 'trump card theology' where the author waits until the end to produce the theological position or argument that appears to win the struggle for Christianity. Which is not to say that I will not want to use Christianity as the primary source for engagement with the other ideas.

As I thought about the possibility of drawing together the different practical and theoretical sources that I have produced in the text, and also what questions might remain unanswered and thus provide material for future debate, it became clear that the notion of governance was a theme running throughout the book. I will offer something of a definition of this shortly but let us just say at this stage that it is about developing ways of establishing codes of practice and public ways of operating that can be used in the increasingly blurred area between the state and what is often called civil society. In an era when either the nation state is more restricted in its powers because of global influences or else the internal political movement is towards rolling back the powers of the state and giving more responsibility to local groups and voluntary bodies, the issue of governance is high on the agenda even though it refers to activity at a series of different levels. I now want to link this to some of the practical involvements I have drawn upon in the book.

In the opening chapter I referred to Local Strategic Partnerships, the idea of social entrepreneurship and the blurred boundary between the welfare state and local church provision of services. While it may be both financially and politically expedient for government to extend its operation to religious and other groupings who work at a more local level, it leaves the question of how such groups are to be monitored and regulated particularly if they are going to be given access to public funds in order to support their work. The notion of social capital, in other words the resources supposedly available from voluntary bodies, and the fact that the government has now established a Faith Communities Unit, both point in the direction of what can be portrayed as a further privatization of welfare provision. One is then left with the question both of the consistency of provision and of the standards and practices that will be found outside formal state provision. Methods of governance, of trying to ensure that non-governmental agencies offering such services can be effectively scrutinized and indeed controlled are going to be crucial to this process. Government may well pay towards the cost of provision but not itself be the provider, in which case it will want to ensure that taxpayers are getting 'value for money' as both the source of finance and as the customers or clients of such services. Governance is a means of trying to guarantee that voluntary groups are seen to be offering a quality service even if at a lower cost.

In chapters two and three I looked in more detail at the theoretical issues that lie behind how we treat those who do not belong to our society or local groupings. The question of gangmasters and the treatment of migrant workers was mentioned. The government is now claiming to be addressing this problem and trying to find ways of monitoring and controlling what happens in this employment sector. The wider subject of human rights is clearly part of this debate. There is no doubt that human rights form a key factor in the task of trying to protect those individuals and groups who are at risk and vulnerable both nationally and globally, and that they are therefore another strategy for addressing the problem of governance at an international level. Potentially this offers a means by which the international community can both monitor and even enforce certain standards of behaviour upon recalcitrant states, although the will to do so is very often determined by other factors both political and economic. Those states who do not adhere to the discourse and practice of human rights can find themselves ostracized and even under direct military threat should those other motivations also exist. Here then we are talking about a means of global governance.

At the very local level I used the examples of the Children's Festival and the Toddlers group to illustrate how questions of identity and community, stimulated by the forces of globalization impinge upon church life, and the resulting ambiguities and dilemmas that arise for those involved. However, even here we did not escape the challenges of justifying our actions to a wider audience and providing reassurance that our practices were acceptable. This meant both constructing a constitution in order to access Lottery funding and also adopting Diocesan Child Protection guidelines in order to cover ourselves as a church-based event. Gone are the days when a group can decide to form itself for a good cause and just get on with the practical tasks. Policies, procedures and other relevant documentation have to be in place before one can request external financial support and reports have to be sent in after the event in order to show that the money has been spent in accordance with the original funding application. This is all now standard practice and has to be appropriately handled within the local group if any activity is to take place. All church work which involves leaving children and young people in the care of adults working on behalf of the church in either a paid or voluntary capacity has to now be subject to Child Protection procedures. There has recently been some controversy over this within the bell-ringing world where some have objected that this requiring of CRB (Criminal Records Bureau) checks for all adults involved is taking a step too far and is likely to diminish even further the numbers of those who might wish to take part. I have also just received notification as Chair of the local school governors that all governors who might wish or need to visit the school during school hours should have an enhanced CRB clearance – and that will have to mean all governors if we are to carry out our responsibilities of visiting the school to monitor its activities and progress. I am also on the Board of Management of a Nightstop project which aims to provide emergency overnight accommodation for 16–25 year olds and in applying for charitable status it has become clear that all Board members require an enhanced CRB clearance even though they may never have direct contact with any of the young people. Whatever one thinks of this level of supervision of voluntary groups it is clearly another example of governance – of trying to establish principles of good practice and codes of conduct which protect all the people involved in the activity.

Within the farming world the levels of government intervention and the bureaucratic demands upon farmers themselves has long been a source of aggravation. Whether this is determined at a national level or is the direct result of the European Common Agricultural Policy does not matter a great deal as the end result is more paper work and administration for the farming community. At an even deeper level questions of environmental protection require legislative frameworks and involve issues of governance. The risks created by environmental problems invariably cross national boundaries in any case and also can be placed at the doorstep of international companies and global interests. There is no doubt that this is one of the major arenas where governance is seen as vital if we are to avoid or contain the potential damage that humans will cause to the planet as a result of continued economic growth. The local example of the Foot and Mouth outbreak perhaps illustrates just how difficult it is to operate codes of practice effectively across a wide variety of contexts where local knowledge and expertise is very rarely taken into account.

My final example is from the Housing Association world where the question of governance is right at the forefront of current discussions. I mentioned in the opening chapter the issue of Board member payment and the controversy that this has caused within the movement. The Housing Corporation, which is the government monitoring body for Housing Associations, has made it quite clear that payment has to be linked to establishing the highest levels of governance within any particular Board. In its document advising Boards on how to proceed it lays out the checklist for action on the subject of good governance. This includes asking questions such as: does the Board perform its key roles well?; does the Board work well together?; does the Board comprise appropriate people?. Its principles of good governance include operating to high ethical standards, accountability to all stakeholders, a spirit of openness including equality of opportunity, a clarity of roles and responsibilities and of course having the proper financial regulations and structures in place. Board members are charged with setting the overall strategy of the organization as well as monitoring performance and attending meetings properly prepared and ready to make a significant contribution. All of this means that Board members themselves should be subject to appraisal and accept being ejected from the Board if they do not perform adequately. Although this does not constitute an employment contract the suggestion is that members sign an agreement accepting their responsibilities before they can take up the post. The role is becoming highly professionalized and requires the highest standards of conduct and performance. This is why the argument that a fee should be offered for the task is now gaining ground. I also have to say that a similar structure is close to being put in place for school governors although what OFSTED require is not yet quite so explicit and there is, of course, no suggestion that school governors be paid for the services they offer. Once again this is about ensuring codes of practice and high standards of behaviour within what is supposedly the voluntary sector brought about largely because government is trying to withdraw while still maintaining a level of control over conduct.

Those are just my examples but there are many others. The issue of corporate governance hit the headlines after the Enron scandal recently and is clearly an area for considerable discussion in its own right but goes beyond the scope of this particular book. Similarly the question of how to regulate international financial institutions is a major political agenda item and there are massive debates surrounding the role of the IMF and the World Bank and their tendency to impose a very restrictive political and economic programme on developing countries. So the list could continue. My point is that governance appears to be a major common theme running through all of my particular involvements as well as touching upon much wider national and international debates on the economy, trade and the environment. How might a Christian perspective be brought to bear on this set of concerns?

The prospects for a Christian encounter

Just as it is the case that each of my practical involvements leads to a concern with the issues of governance it can also be argued that the theoretical resources upon which I have drawn could throw light upon aspects of a Christian encounter with this question. In a sense this is the beginning of another substantial piece of work and all I can do is to offer some pointers towards a developing programme of research. My initial response to this whole area of debate is that all the talk about governance creates a series of unrealistic expectations about what can be achieved by such means. I will attempt to articulate these concerns.

I have already pointed out earlier in the text my worries about what can sensibly be expected of volunteers in the current economic and social climate. There is certainly an issue of appropriate expertise and the problem of non-professionals being expected to make strategic judgements in areas where their knowledge is more limited than that of the professionals for whom they are taking responsibility. I experience this regularly in the Housing Association world and indeed as a school governor. If I reverse the situation and imagine somebody from those worlds coming into my arena of professional competence – e.g. theology, pastoral care or the conduct of worship – with an expectation that they would hold a responsible brief for how I conduct my 'business' and set out a strategy for the future let alone monitor my performance, I think I would be somewhat hesitant in what I might expect of them. I acknowledge that significant lay people within parishes do constantly play an important role in shaping what work develops and participate in that, but there are still areas where I would always want to back my professional judgement and not be 'governed' by the well-meaning amateur. Thus if I was the Chief Executive of a large housing group with the responsibilities and the salary to match I can imagine that I could well both resent and resist the 'interference' of outsiders who do not really understand the business. I have to give enormous credit to the people in the Housing Association world with whom I have worked that they have not made me feel like that at all but appear to share the responsibilities with openness and good grace. So perhaps my fears are unfounded or perhaps it is simply that Board members do build up a body of knowledge and expertise over time that can earn them the trust and respect of the professionals. Or perhaps it is that good professionals learn how to handle Board members and make them feel that they are more powerful than they really are!

There is a further fraught issue of the involvement of 'customers' on Boards whether we are talking about parent governors for schools or tenant Board members for Housing Associations. Here we encounter some extremely blurred boundaries which anybody would find it difficult to hold firm. When personal interests and concerns are at stake questions of confidentiality let alone objective judgement inevitably come to the fore. Again this is not to say that individuals do not handle such tensions with integrity and a proper 'professionalism', but to point out that there are real dilemmas and tensions which arise as a result of crossing this boundary. The question of volunteer motivation and thus the basis for social capital is also at stake here. There is always the suspicion that a number of people who do choose to get involved do so because they have a personal interest, so, for instance, as long as one has a child at the school it is deemed reasonable to be a governor or a member of the PTA but of course once that ceases to be the case one's interests shift elsewhere and the commitment is not sustained. Perhaps this is fine but it does leave questions of the sustainability of such activity and the extent to which commitment does stem from personal interest rather than from some more altruistic motive. So once again there may be greater limitations on this sort of engagement with governance activities than we often acknowledge. Also, the more demanding such activity becomes, the more 'professionalized' and structured, the more difficult it may become to encourage people to participate at all. Who would be a volunteer these days?

This is inevitably related to the issues of identity and community that I raised in chapters 4 and 5. On the one hand individuals and families are under pressure to perform at a high level in their own professional capacity leaving less time available for local involvement and commitment, living with the fear of redundancy or career change and the financial consequences of that let alone of the decisions about schooling that are now so important. In the culture of personal choice where one competes with those around to achieve both oneself and through one's children, commitment to local provision is bound to take second place to obtaining the best quality service provision to which one can afford to gain access. What priority is going to be placed on local voluntary activity when these other competing factors are now so important? Yet running alongside this is the unspoken need to create the local groupings or enclaves of interim intimacy that supposedly compensate for the loss of real 'community' that now accompanies the global lifestyle. As I have argued, churches all too readily step into the breach here believing that this is still the old-fashioned commitment to church and community when it is in fact a new animal or hybrid version and without realizing how quickly people will walk away from the commitment once it no longer fits with their personal agenda. In this environment how are people going to be persuaded to participate in structures of governance at a local level? They are both consumers of services in one part of their lives and then also responsible for the delivery of services in others and this is another source of potential internal conflict.

A further concern that I have is that putting such governance structures in place at whatever level – international, national or local – will itself offer an unrealistic reassurance that all will now be well and that we can stop worrying about whatever issue is being addressed. We know from bitter experience that this is far from being the case. The failure of Child Protection procedures to prevent adults gaining access to children when they should not do so is a constant problem. This will be replayed in other ways across the spectrum. Simply having the correct policies and structures in place will not, in itself, prevent the abuses and mistakes that human beings regularly make, although it might convince insurers that all necessary precautions have been taken. Yet if we ignore the requirement for governance there appear to be no alternative methods for regulating the activities within civil society. So I would have to conclude that governance is both essential and yet inadequate for performing the tasks expected of it. We cannot do without it, but neither must we expect it to 'deliver the goods' of good practice and acceptable behaviour.

There is a deeper level at which I believe we need to address this tension and I can best express this by returning to the work of Habermas. As I have already said, what concerns me about the discourse of governance is that it is overly rationalistic and thus reflects what appears to be a cultural tendency to suggest that once all the appropriate external structures are in place one can be optimistic about the possibilities of success. If there is a good governing body at the local school, for instance, one can then reasonably expect that all will be well and service delivery will leave nothing to be desired. This does not take into account the essential indeterminacy of people's lives and also suggests that what is demanded is a completed product rather than a commitment to improve and refine what are inevitably flawed organizations. Once again there is the danger of encouraging a consumerist mentality even though that is contradicted by one's experience of oneself as an incomplete human being. This optimism and unrealistic expectation of what can be achieved is evident in some of Habermas's recent writing on the theme of governance.

Habermas's main concern is with governance at the international level. Now that the nation state cannot control concerns about the environment or the movement of international trade or finance, the question emerges of how these are going to be addressed. There are two alternatives, either some form of international or global government or instead a trust in networks of governance that are now emerging. These take many forms including social movements, non-governmental organizations, regional government and groups established through the Internet. Habermas favours these as being able to influence decision-making processes and setting the boundaries within which governments and international organizations can legitimately operate. This is essentially a dispersal of power between different agencies which can all have a part to play in the public arena and also builds upon his theory of communicative reason.

> In short, governance denotes a method for dealing with political controversies in which actors, political and non-political, arrive at mutually acceptable decisions by deliberating and negotiating with each other. It is based on a variety of processes with different authority bases, and highlights the role of voluntary and non-profit organizations in joint decision-making and implementation and the semi-public character of modern political enterprise. (Erikson and Weigard 2003, 250–51)

However, there are problems and constraints with such a model. Does it really mean that ordinary people do not in fact have access to the decision-making procedures since the real relationship is between the particular individuals on the governance bodies and the executives who are still 'running the show'? This may indeed represent an effective way of making decisions but it seems somewhat distant from the model of popular democracy that Habermas has always claimed to espouse. Is there genuine accountability to service users and those whose lives will be affected by such decisions? This is a tension that I feel within the Housing Association world where Boards are becoming ever more professionalized and business-orientated and thus distant from tenants and local communities. There is the possibility that what is being created is another layer of executive control merely disguised under the rhetoric of governance and remote from those who are the customers of the business. The interests of the non-executive directors on the Board are ever more likely to coincide with those of senior management as the organization grows into another sort of enterprise. Similarly with Habermas's hopes for the effectiveness of intermediate bodies, how democratic can they be if they too become more closely drawn into the power networks that they might have been set up to resist and challenge? How easy will it be for 'outsiders' to gain access to the guardians of integrity and good practice when they too are so influenced by the culture that they are there to monitor and critique? It seems to me that Habermas, with his background in the Enlightenment tradition of a reformulated reason and democratic liberal politics, has an inflated view of what governance can achieve. Yet, unless there is something like this how can there be any checks and balances on the exercise of power at these levels?

For me this returns now to the underlying discussion about the relationship between faith and reason. If we place governance under the heading of reason, one is left with the question of how – if at all – the insights of a faith tradition might relate to this developing and significant arena of social action. Is it simply that the two are alien traditions and that Christianity must say that it rests upon an unjustifiably optimistic view of human nature in which it is argued that if we can get the structures and processes right the worst human excesses can be prevented in public life? If so then there will be no significant engagement with what is clearly a very important set of practical issues and Christians will be forced to stand apart and criticize from the sidelines. At the other extreme, if faith communities are willing and eager to be drawn further into the issues of welfare provision under the tempting heading of social capital, then there could be a naïve and unrealistic expectation of what might be achieved and some very big disappointments to follow. Even more seriously there could be a complete failure to recognize some of the deep-seated tensions and conflicts over values that already underpin this debate and the danger of 'being eaten' or appropriated by a set of cultural beliefs that require critical scrutiny to say the least. Where is faith to stand in this particular relationship with reason?

I have been arguing throughout the text for the possibility of another set of relationships based upon a number of locations for encounter between faith and reason. It is crucial to understand this clearly. I believe that the relationships are always already potentially in place because elements of what we call reason embody components of what we know as faith and vice versa. Faith is evident within the optimistic expectations of governance as reason is at work within the thought-processes and arguments encountered within Christian communities. Hence it is not a matter of criticizing reason by applying to it an external principle that bears no relationship to other discussions. The notion of deconstruction that I still find helpful suggests rather that it is the 'other' that is already within the original that can be brought to the surface and display another possible relationship. This is one major contribution of the work of Derrida and Levinas to this whole discussion. The 'other' is already within the concept and the practice of governance and can then provide the basis for a significant engagement between the two traditions.

At this point I want to return to the more theological ideas that form the core of this book. How does governance stand judged by the four criteria that I have suggested form the basis of such a relationship? Does it acknowledge the tension between the universal and the particular? Is there a messianic dimension to its values or is it simply rooted in the here and now? Does it embody an understanding of human subjectivity that includes both the pre-autonomous and post-autonomous dimensions? Can it take account of the essential indeterminacy of social and political life or does it build upon a deterministic and static view of how things work? Even if governance so far appears to fail according to some or all of these criteria is that the end of the story or should Christians now be attempting to build those missing components into the concept through a critical and constructive engagement including practical activities?

On the first of those criteria it seems clear that the tension between the universal and the particular cuts right through most governance issues whether they are at the international, national or local level. My fear would be that the tendency would be to emphasize the universal or more general at the expense of the local. Whether we are thinking about the domain of human rights or down at the most basic level with the monitoring of church bell ringing groups it is hard to see how the generalized concerns represented by governance can take account of or do justice to individual or local circumstances. The levels of administration and bureaucracy required for such monitoring procedures inevitably obscure both detail and difference. Everybody in a particular category must conform to certain standards of behaviour and performance whatever the particular situation. There seems little scope for flexibility or discretion in most of the governance measures that I have encountered. Whether this is something that could realistically be challenged by local groups, religious or otherwise, is perhaps doubtful. However, if Christianity is indeed always concerned for the particular, the individual or group who does not fit into the wider category, it must be wary of such processes and of the dangers of subsuming what is indeed different beneath an all-consuming category. This may mean standing apart and criticizing from the outside but also the possibility of having to be involved and therefore being drawn into governance procedures in which case it must find ways of retaining its critical perspective. The only way to work this out would be to examine specific cases which is beyond the scope of this present text.

Is there a messianic dimension to governance? Again it may be difficult to see how there could be since governance procedures are primarily preoccupied with dealing with things as they are and attempting to ensure acceptable standards of practice and codes of behaviour. Yet unless there is some horizon or target towards which governance is aiming then there could be no basis for its critique of current practice. It is not just aimed at keeping things in check but also has the objective of improving and striving towards higher standards. Perhaps this seems too broad or bland a suggestion to count as being messianic, but it may form the beginning of a discussion if nothing else. After all the purpose of identifying the four locations for the encounter between faith and reason was not to show that they are actually the same thing, but rather to suggest areas where there might be enough common ground to make it worthwhile initiating a discussion. The ideals and objectives of the Christian tradition will always be that much more demanding and even utopian but there may still be some connection with the ideals embedded in governance as and when it operates most effectively. Corporate governance for instance has already struck resonances in the minds of some who have a concern for spirituality. Should a company build into its core objectives criteria about concern for the environment, for the working conditions of its employees, for good relationships with customers and local communities and so on? Hence a messianic location for encounter may not be so far-fetched after all.

In terms of the criterion of acknowledging the pre- and post-autonomous dimensions of human subjectivity it is difficult to be too optimistic and this may well be the area where religious traditions need to concentrate their critical efforts. If governance is a form of rationality and works on the assumption that if certain procedures are followed then good or appropriate results are guaranteed then one would want to propose that it rests on a limited view of what it is to be a human being. It may be both over-optimistic in the level of change that it believes can be expected in human behaviour but also unduly pessimistic in the ideal of what human beings might become according to the Christian tradition. It may fail to take into account the extent to which humans are determined or conditioned by both internal and external factors and cannot therefore be simply manipulated or guided into alternative patterns. However it may also expect too little of humanity by restricting its vision to a compliance with rather mundane codes of practice. There would not be enough that would count as messianic then or the striving for an open identity or post-autonomous dimension. Once again one would need to examine the working of particular governance measures in greater detail in order to substantiate this claim.

Finally on the issue of indeterminacy and democracy there is also much yet to be achieved and established. The notion that setting particular procedures in motion would achieve the desired objectives fails to take account of the indeterminacy of human life and behaviour, although it is hard to see how one can avoid hoping that such might be the case. We have also raised the question in the discussion of Habermas's view of whether those who are drawn into governance are in any way representative and indeed whether or not this is important. This is a major question within the political debates surrounding governance and requires a more detailed exposition that I would hope to pursue on another occasion.

Throughout the text I have been examining a whole series of blurred encounters that result from direct engagement between the Christian tradition and a range of social and community based activities. I have also argued that such engagement cannot avoid the risk of Christian values being appropriated or compromised. However, using Derrida's analogy of being eaten I have attempted to show that it is possible to establish criteria by which we might judge whether or not we are being 'eaten well'. I hope by now that it is clear that the four criteria that I have developed as a result of the work to establish another relationship between faith and reason have considerable value across a series of involvements from the local to the global. As I draw the text to a close perhaps it is worth suggesting that the concept of governance might have an application here as well. As long as one accepts the limitations of this language, one could argue that the four criteria: the tension between the universal and the particular; the messianic dimension of human activity; the search for a post-autonomous or open identity within the realm of subjectivity and finally the recognition of the indeterminacies involved in public life, do provide some rules of engagement or 'governance' for the relationship between the Christian tradition and the secular-dominated spheres of the social and political worlds. This is not to say that all or any of these locations for encounter would have to be present if such blurred boundaries are to be a comfortable place to be, but rather that this is more likely to be the case if one or more of these locations were to be identified. This does not in itself solve any problems or resolve any of the tensions, but it might help Christians to feel justified in staying with the issues concerned in the hope that appropriate consequences might follow from such engagement. After all, the alternative to taking the risks is simply to remain behind the barricades and dream

133

that, one day, the rest of the world will choose to come inside. I do not believe that we can afford to wait that long. I also believe that the message of the Christian tradition is that we need to work towards that open identity or post-autonomous dimension that is part of the messianic vision that has been presented to us and that this is more likely to happen as we become involved in the world as it is. The price we have to pay for this may be the willingness to lose our integrity and identity in the service of a greater cause.

Glossary

Acquiescing to the testimony of the other

This is a phrase used by Derrida building upon the ideas of Levinas and suggesting that there is a prior need to accept views and assumptions 'on trust', perhaps because of respect for or on the authority of another person or a tradition, before the process of argumentation can begin. Thus, for instance, what we call 'faith' and 'reason' BOTH rely on acquiescing to the testimony of the other to some degree. This is also to establish that there is a pre-autonomous dimension to human subjectivity (see below).

Autonomy – pre-autonomy and post-autonomy

The Enlightenment concept of autonomy proposes that individuals can exercise independent judgement and thus escape the influences of both traditions and other people. Using the ideas of Derrida and Levinas as above I argue that this concept needs to be expanded to take into account both the pre-autonomous and post-autonomous dimensions. The pre-autonomous is the recognition that all arguments start somewhere and have to rest on assumptions that are adopted for reasons that may not be immediately justifiable or open to critical examination – although they may subsequently become subject to criticism. Post-autonomy is more elusive and difficult to articulate and draws upon Irigaray's hints at new forms of autonomy, Castells's search for a project identity and my own view that there is a messianic dimension to human subjectivity. In Christian terms we do not yet know who we are or what we shall be so 'identity' remains a horizon as much as a present achievement.

Colonization of the lifeworld

This is a term coined by Habermas to describe the ways in which the values of the Systems World e.g. of commerce, finance and big business, increasingly impinge upon and appropriate areas of human life previously determined by the background values of the lifeworld. By the latter Habermas is thinking of the sphere of the family and of normal social life including the realm of religion. This 'colonization' is a result of the predominance of an instrumental reason and can only be countered by his alternative of communicative reason (see below). An example of this as referred to in the text would be competitive and commercial values playing an increased role in the world of education or of housing provision. Rather than sending their children to the nearest school parents will now exercise choice based on their perceptions of the quality of education on offer and of 'value for money'.

Communicative reason

Communicative reason is Habermas's alternative to the narrowing influence of what is called instrumental reason or a 'means-ends' rationality. He proposes his concept as the appropriate heir to the Enlightenment tradition claiming that it can take into account both context and the ideas of particular traditions. Hence it supposedly encapsulates both the 'particular' and the 'universal' thus dealing with one of the major points of tension within any interpretation of reason. The universal dimension of communicative reason is based on a theory of language as communication within which Habermas identifies four criteria by which we can evaluate effective communication: understanding; truth; truthfulness and normative correctness. In the text I argue that Habermas does not fully succeed in the objective of doing justice to all possible 'particulars' but that, nevertheless, something like this concept is essential if we are not to abandon any form of reason.

Contextual theology

This is a relatively recent development in theology that claims to place equal or greater weight upon engagement with context as upon the more commonly recognized sources of theology i.e. Scripture, Tradition and Reason. Perhaps the earliest public form of this was Liberation Theology emerging from the context of Latin America and using tools of Marxist analysis. However, since then there have been many other versions of contextual theologies including my own *Local Theology* developed from within a deep rural UK setting. Although this idea has now been taken up within academic theology with the development of courses and textbooks, in my view it remains an essentially engaged approach based upon the practice of people within a particular context. It raises the question of the relationship between the 'particular' and 'universal' within theology and thus parallels the same debate within philosophy of which Habermas's work is a prime example.

Deconstruction

This is the term made famous (or infamous) by Derrida and requires very circumspect handling because it has been subject to a whole range of misunderstandings. Amongst these are the suggestion that it means the indiscriminate and arbitrary destruction of meaning through a free-for-all of interpretation where anything can be made to mean anything. This is not the case with Derrida's own work which always displays very rigorous and detailed expositions of particular texts. However, neither is deconstruction an identifiable or universal technique of interpretation that can be applied to texts in a mechanical way. My own understanding of it, following Derrida as best I can, is that it reveals the other that always lies hidden within a text. Once an interpretation becomes accepted certain other possibilities are then ruled out or left aside. Deconstruction destabilizes this stabilization of interpretation not in order to argue that the meaning of a text needs to be reversed but in order to highlight the other possibilities that still retain a validity of their own. Its value then is in 'releasing the subversive other' and so potentially establishing a critique of the power at work in all interpretation. In terms of this book I am arguing that if 'faith' is indeed one of the 'others' of 'reason' then there is the possibility of another relationship between them based on the four criteria that I identify in chapter 3.

Deliberative democracy

This is a development of the ideas of participatory democracy building upon the work of Habermas amongst others and arguing that all those who are likely to be affected by a particular decision should have a say in its formulation. This would establish the legitimacy of the political process more effectively than the forms of representative democracy which are now dominant.

Discourse ethics

Discourse ethics is Habermas's expansion of his concept of communicative reason into the field of morality. As with his other key ideas such as deliberative democracy it presupposes that the validity of positions adopted and decisions reached depends upon the full and open participation of all those who have an interest or a stake in the process – in this case the development of ethical stances.

Enclave of interim intimacy

This is a phrase that I use in the text to describe the way in which people who no longer have direct access to the former structures of community life actively seek out and construct a substitute that relies upon close and yet fragile relationships. Increased social mobility, enhanced working pressures and subsequent uncertainty and distance from family support networks, each created or exacerbated by the forces of the global economy, all contribute to the formation of such enclaves. Local churches and community groups readily collude in constructing these enclaves without necessarily recognizing that they are 'for the time being only' and may potentially undermine the older 'community values' of reciprocity and commitment to locality.

Globalization

According to Held (Held 2004, 1), globalization 'at its simplest refers to a shift or transformation in the scale of human organization that links distant communities and expands the reach of power across the world's regions'. This greater interconnectedness creates both problems and new possibilities. I am particularly concerned in this book with the impact of globalization upon families and local communities. For instance once family members start commuting around the world for reasons of either business or leisure they have less time and energy available to give to either individual or community commitment raising doubts about the sustainability of existing social patterns and institutions.

Governance

Governance is possibly becoming a term that is as equally contested and complicated as 'globalization'. It often refers to the setting and management of the rules of conduct of all forms of public organization, although these can be international, national or local. It involves issues of trust, reciprocity, authority and accountability. As I reviewed the practical issues that I have described in the text I concluded that governance is a theme running throughout and would now want to pursue the possibility of establishing a critical Christian engagement with this notion using the four criteria established in chapter 3. In particular I am concerned about the level of expectation of what can be achieved by governance and also the ways in which power is exercised within such rules of conduct.

Institutional individualism

Institutional individualism is Beck's way of describing how individuals are now 'set adrift' from the older structures of family, community and religious traditions and are forced to make key decisions about their lives without uncritical reference to such resources. This is an explicit critique of the more commonly accepted concept of individualism as a 'me-first', 'every man or woman for themselves', self-centred version of contemporary social life. It thus contrasts starkly with most Christian criticisms of current social trends as being based on a selfish and consumerist form of individualism. According to Beck we have no choice now but to construct our lives and personal biographies from the shattered remains of the old traditions and of accepting the risks of making bad decisions in the knowledge that the former structures of family, community or Welfare State will not be there to 'pick up the pieces' if we get it wrong. Pension provision or that for the further education of new born babies are both excellent examples of these sorts of life decisions. Our 'bricolage biographies' carry enormous uncertainties with them and can again encourage the construction of enclaves of interim intimacy as a reaction against this – a temporary haven where we are sheltered from the consequences of institutional individualism.

Instrumental reason

This form of reason is what Critical Theorists such as Habermas suggest is the distortion of the Enlightenment tradition into a narrow 'means-ends' rationality. Within this, reason becomes the slave to purely mechanical and potentially inhuman objectives and leads to Weber's 'iron cage of bureaucracy' or even to the horrors of the Holocaust (Bauman). Reason can be rescued from this fate, according to Habermas, by developing the alternative of a communicative reason.

Liquid modernity

Liquid modernity is a term coined by Bauman to articulate the essential fluidity and temporary nature of social and political life. Within these spheres everything is now 'for the time being only' as individuals change jobs, locations, relationships, commitments and even identities with increasing regularity. The older structures and resources (solids) still survive, but their role in shaping and securing peoples' lives is undermined and they become another consumer item to be discarded and discredited at will. New forms of church life and worship e.g. our Toddlers service, are now displaying 'liquid' characteristics raising the question of whether they will supplement or undermine the 'solid' structures and institutions of religious traditions.

Mediated singularities

If we recall the episode of Abraham and his potential sacrifice of Isaac it is possible to argue that the moment of encounter with God is so unique and outside other human experience as to be 'beyond articulation'. One could say then that the depth of religious experience is a singularity, a point in time and action that escapes all attempts to place it within any code of either ethics or any language game. However, if such experiences are to be communicated to others or turned into structures with which others can engage then they will have to be 'mediated' through language. Thus the discourse of faith, its symbols, liturgies and doctrines can be seen as 'mediated singularities' and acknowledged as being unable to do justice to any original experience of or encounter with the divine.

Messianic

Derrida formulates the idea of the messianic as a way of describing a structure of human existence – waiting for the 'Messiah' to arrive – that is related to and yet not dependent upon the specific messianisms of Islam, Judaism and Christianity. Hence, he suggests, concepts such as democracy, justice and human rights can be seen to have a messianic dimension. We continue to await and hope for their arrival, but in the knowledge that we would probably not recognize them even if they were to appear. Also any claims to have 'achieved' democracy etc. thus need to be carefully scrutinized as possible crude disguises for the exercise of power. The point is that the 'Messiah' in any form is always still to come.

Post-Foundational

A Post-Foundational approach to theology challenges the view that it is appropriate to envisage theology as a building or solid structure based upon the secure and incontrovert-ible foundations of Scripture, Tradition or Reason. Rather it is more appropriately seen as a process or even a network of possible connections, thus acknowledging that all human attempts to articulate the divine are both contingent and fallible. This is not to deny that the sources formerly seen as foundations are still important but to argue that their role within the formation of the tradition is now more fluid and flexible. In *Beyond All Reason* I used the idea of mediating frameworks to suggest ways in which the resources of the Christian tradition might relate to resources from other disciplines based on this more fluid understanding and also argued that Christianity, like all other traditions, is better seen as a major narrative than a metanarrative in response to the challenge of postmodernity. This parallels the term 'Post-Metaphysical' within philosophy which does not necessarily claim that we have now reached the 'end' of metaphysics but rather that we must now see such ideas in a new light. There are also resonances with the views of Bauman and Beck on the formerly solid and secure structures of individual and social life.

Project identity

This term is taken from the work of Castells on the rise of the network society and proposes that there is an alternative to the resistance identity that is becoming the predominant reaction to the forces of global capitalism. It links clearly with my notion of post-autonomy in suggesting that some people are in the process of forging new identities that are no longer simply shaped by existing traditions nor forming their identities by belonging to 'communities of resistance' or enclaves of interim intimacy as a reaction to or escape from the uncertainties created by globalization. He sees New Social Movements such as feminism and environmental groups as possible breeding grounds for such project identities but does not limit his interests exclusively to these.

Social capital

The classic definition of this is 'features of social organization, such as trust, norms, and networks, that can improve the efficiency of society by facilitating coordinated actions' (Putnam quoted in Anne Mette Kjaer 2004, 160). Once again the growing interest in this concept represents the requirement of governments to be able to draw upon the voluntary sector and civil society more generally in order to support welfare provision. Churches and other religious groups are seen as a prime source of social capital, particularly within more deprived communities and thus become targets for government funding but also for governance procedures. Whether or not they should become involved in this way is an important question and another of the blurred boundaries examined in this book.

Social enterprise

This concept emerges from the increased blurring of the boundary between voluntary action and the commercial sector and the very practical need to access private funding for social initiatives. A major concern within the voluntary sector is for the sustainability of projects which are very often only funded for the short term and unable to generate their own income over time. Social enterprise is a means of encouraging such projects to use commercial methods in order to increase their viability and to become less dependent upon initial capital funding. Whether this will lead to the compromise of the values and ethos of voluntary action is very much an open question as I suggest in the text.

Stock Transfer Housing Associations

Stock Transfer Housing Associations were initiated in the early 1990s as a means of circumventing the then Conservative Government policy on social housing that prevented local authorities building any new properties. If the tenants of a local authority voted by a simply majority to transfer their properties to a newly-formed housing association with Board members representing the Local Authority, tenants and local community and business interests, then this became a way of accessing private funding, invariably banks or building societies, in order to both improve the existing stock and also begin a development programme. One could see this as a semi-privatization of Local Authority Housing and a forerunner of the Private Finance Initiative. As such it was initially opposed by many Labour controlled councils. However, a high proportion of social housing is now in the hands of such housing associations or registered social landlords and the sector has become increasingly commercialized and subject to competitive and business interests. Those of us directly involved would argue that this has been to the benefit of tenants and lead to both better housing stock and to new developments. However, the increased withdrawal of government subsidy to such enterprises has created significant pressures on the financing of such bodies and led to a round of mergers and 'partnerships' the longer term consequences of which remain unpredictable.

The Saying and the Said

A key phrase used by Levinas to point to the tension between the singularity of the religious experience or encounter and the need to articulate these in order to communicate them to others. The Saying is the direct encounter which escapes full articulation and the Said is the formulation of this in discourse which becomes the development of a tradition and enables others to relate to it without necessarily having had the original experience. The residue of the Saying – that which escapes or eludes the process of articulation – needs to be made present again in order to 'deconstruct' the stable interpretations which so quickly form a new orthodoxy within any tradition. Without this the 'other' which is the divine risks being reduced to a set of formulae or concepts which can never do justice to the original encounter. I would want to link this to a Post-Foundational and a contextual approach to theology.

Bibliography

Atherton, J.
  2003   *Marginalization*, SCM Press, London.

Bauman, Z.
  1991   *Modernity and the Holocaust*, Polity Press, Cambridge.
  2000   *Liquid Modernity*, Polity Press, Cambridge.

Beck, U. and Beck-Gernsheim, E.
  2002   *Individualization: Institutionalized individualism and its social and political consequences*, Sage Publications, London.

Bohman, J. and Rehg, W. (eds.)
  1997   *Deliberative Democracy: Essays on reason and politics*, Massachusetts Institute of Technology, London.

Caputo, John D.
  1997   *The Prayers and Tears of Jacques Derrida: Religion without reason*, Indiana University Press, Bloomington and Indianapolis, USA.
  1998   *On Religion*, Routledge, London.

Caputo, John D. and Scanlon, Michael J. (eds.)
  1999   *God, the Gift and Postmodernism*, Indiana University Press, Bloomington and Indianapolis, USA.

Castells, M.
  1997   'The Power of Identity: the Information Age', in *Economy, Culture and Society*, Volume 11, Blackwell, Oxford.

Critchley, S.
  1998   The Ethics of Deconstruction: Derrida and Levinas, Edinburgh University Press.

Critchley, S. and Bernasconi, R.
  2002   *The Cambridge Companion to Levinas*, Cambridge University Press.

Derrida, J.
  1995   *The Gift of Death*, University of Chicago Press, London.
  1996   in Chantal Mouffe (ed.) *Deconstruction and Pragmatism*, Simon Critchley, Jacques Derrida, Ernesto Laclau and Richard Rorty, Routledge, London.
  1997   *Writing and Difference*, Routledge, London.
  1999   *Adieu: to Emmanuel Levinas*, Stanford University Press, Stanford, California, USA.

Derrida, J. and Vattimo, G.
  1998   *Religion*, Polity Press, Cambridge.

Deutscher, P.
  2002   *A Politics of Impossible Difference: The later work of Luce Irigaray*, Cornell University Press, Cornell, USA.

Douzanis, C.
2000   *The End of Human Rights*, Hart Publishing, Oxford.
Erikson, E. and Weigard, J.
2003   *Understanding Habermas*, Continuum, London.
Habermas, J.
1984   *The Theory of Communicative Action: Volume 1: Reason and the rationalization of society*, Heinemann, London.
1987   *The Theory of Communicative Action: Volume 2: The critique of functionalist reason*, Polity Press, Cambridge.
1992   *Moral Consciousness and Communicative Action*, Polity Press, Cambridge.
Held, D.
2004   *Global Covenant: The social democratic alternative to the Washington consensus*, Polity Press, Cambridge.
Irigaray, L.
1996   *I Love to You*, Routledge, London.
2000a   *To be Two*, The Athlone Press, London.
2000b   *Why Different?*, Semiotext, Columbia University, USA.
Kjear, A.M.
2004   *Governance*, Polity Press, Cambridge.
Levinas, E.
1969   *Totality and Infinity: An essay on exteriority*, Dusquesne University Press, Pittsburgh, Pennsylvania, USA.
1981   *Otherwise Than Being*, Dusquesne University Press, Pittsburgh, Pennsylvania. USA.
Llewelyn, J.
1991   *The Middle Voice of Ecological Conscience*, Macmillan, London.
New Economics Foundation, Church Urban Fund.
2001   *Faith, Hope and Participation*, Church Urban Fund, London.
Olthius, J.H. (ed.)
2002   *Religion with/out Religion: The prayers and tears of John D. Caputo*, Routledge, London.
Reader, J.
1994   *Local Theology: Church and community in dialogue*, SPCK, London.
1997   *Beyond All Reason: The limits of postmodern theology*, Aureus, Cardiff.
2002   *The Problem of Faith and Reason after Habermas and Derrida*, unpublished Ph.D. thesis with University of Wales, Bangor.
2004   'Deconstructing Autonomy: towards a new identity', in *Ecotheology*, 9.2.
Scase, R. and Scales, J.
2003   *Regional Futures and Neighbourhood Realities*, National Housing Federation, London.
Watson, B.G.
2004   *Truth and Scripture: Challenging underlying assumptions*, Aureus, Cardiff.

Index

143